Membership Development:

101 Ways To Get and Keep Your Members!

by
Mark Levin, CAE

ISBN 0-9660080-0-6

First Printing, February, 1996
Second Printing, September, 1996
Third Printing, January, 1997
Fourth Printing, M~~ ^1997^
Fifth Printing, M
Six Printing, Decer
Seventh Printing,]

B.A.I., Inc.

9891 Broken Land Parkway
Suite 300
Columbia, MD 21046
Ph: 301-596-2584
Fax: 301-596-2594

For
Barbara Ann

c'mere, rouge

Spreading the Wealth

In 1986, the Carol Jean Cancer Foundation was established to provide a place for children with cancer to go for recreation and support. These children, ages 3-17, spend a week free of charge at Camp Friendship, where they and their families get enjoyment out of doing all the things that children without this disease get to enjoy every day.

A portion of the purchase price of each copy of **101 Ways to Get and Keep Your Members** goes directly to the Carol Jean Cancer Foundation to support efforts to bring an extra portion of love and happiness to the children.

For more information on the Carol Jean Cancer Foundation and Camp Friendship, call 301-587-6300.

Table of Contents

Page

Introduction

MEMBERSHIP IS FOREVER

It's amazing!

No matter how long I've been in this field and no matter how many organizations I work with, the question I get asked most frequently is always the same: "What is the biggest issue facing not-for-profit organizations?"

As we get closer to the twenty-first century the question is changed only slightly to "What do you think will be the biggest issue for not-for-profit organizations in the next century?"

It's the same question I've heard for 25 years and the answer I give is the same one I've given for those 25 years. The most important issue facing associations, societies, chambers of commerce and other not-for-profit organizations is **membership.**

My first assignment after entering the association management field in 1970 was as the assistant executive director for a local chapter of the Boy Scouts of America. I was responsible for leadership development, training, publications' sales, chapter development, and above all, membership recruitment and retention. Recruit new members and learn how to keep them and you'll have a great career, I was told by my supervisor.

He was right.

When interviewing with the Scouts for my next position as a chapter director - a position that gave me more responsibility and staff - the first question I was asked by the volunteer search committee was "Can you help us gain more members?" I could, and I did.

I moved on to become regional membership director for the Associated Builders and Contractors (ABC). ABC is a major construction trade association with over 15,000 corporate members in 80 chapters throughout the United States. My supervisor told me that the only reason I got the job was my track record in membership. Within two years I became ABC's national membership director and managed a department with three Regional Membership Directors, two interns and a support staff in ABC's Washington, D.C. headquarters. I got that job because of my success in membership development, too. Every month I attended the meeting of ABC's executive committee where the members discussed education, government relations, conventions, planning, financial matters and everything else related to the effective leadership of the association. The first question asked by these volunteer leaders every month was "How are we doing in membership?" They realized that the success of all these other programs depended upon our success in membership.

During my six years in that department ABC's membership did quite well.

I then spent six years as an account executive for an association management firm. My assignment there was to serve as executive director for two international associations and one national association with 23 chapters. Talk about issues! These groups dealt with everything from writing international technical standards to putting on product promotion programs and major trade shows. The volunteer boards of directors of these organizations consisted of people who ran major international corporations as well as people who were worried about making a profit in small, family-owned businesses. The issues facing these organizations had a direct impact on the livelihood of everyone in their respective fields. Without exception the first question I was asked during my first board meeting for each organization was "Can you help us grow?" Once again, I said I could and I did.

In 1986 I started my own company, B.A.I., Inc. My goal was then, and continues to be, to use my experience in association and not-for-profit management to help other organizations grow and prosper. Since starting B.A.I., I've worked with hundreds of chambers of commerce, trade associations, professional societies and other organizations all over the world trying to help them deal with what they perceived to be their biggest issue - membership. I've also worked with or to spoken to tens of thousands of volunteer leaders and organizational staff members about membership recruitment and retention. These experiences have allowed me to help others and at the same time to learn from them. Their successes and failures add to the ideas and information I share with other organizations. In my current role as Executive Vice President of the Chain Link Fence Manufacturers Institute, I face the same day-to-day membership issues as my client organizations do. So, the ideas I pick up from others are put into practice right away. As I travel around the world working with not-for-profit organizations, I find that membership is a universal topic. At a meeting held in Santiago, Chile for the executive directors of 26 chambers of commerce in Latin America, the topic of choice was membership development. In my work helping to bring about changes in developing democracies in Africa, the volunteer and staff leaders from newly-formed associations and chambers said their most pressing issue wasn't programming or government interaction, it was membership development.

Even when the topic isn't membership it is still on everyone's mind. When I held a series of training programs for the Australian Society of Association Executives, the topic was supposed to be creating a better working relationship between staff and volunteer leaders. I asked the attendees if there was one aspect of this broad topic they most wanted to cover and several attendees wanted to spend time talking about getting and keeping members!

My views on membership are not based solely on my experiences as a staff person and consultant. I've also been a member of two chambers of commerce, two trade associations, one convention bureau, and five professional societies. The suggestions I make to individuals and organizations about what they can do to attract and keep more members are based just as much on my views as a member of organizations as they are on my experiences as a staff person.

Whether I'm teaching membership or learning about it, I always find membership work to be one of the most challenging and exciting parts of my career. Whether working as a local chapter person in the 1970s or as an international speaker and consultant in the 1990s, I find membership is always the issue.

It's amazing.

USING THE BOOK

This book was written to share my experiences and viewpoint with others facing the important issue of membership. I tried to avoid using words and phrases that make assumptions about your (the reader's) background or experience. One phrase that <u>will</u> be new is *Levin's Basic Law of Membership Development.*. This law simply states that in almost all cases your organization's ability to get and keep members is based on three things: being able to personalize membership for the member, being able to customize the recruitment and retention process, and being able to have and express empathy for members and prospective members.

To make using the book as easy as possible the chapters have been formatted in a very special way. At the beginning of each chapter, there is a short list of what will be covered and what you can expect to take away from that chapter. At the end of each chapter there is a summary entitled "Lessons Learned" that will highlight the key points in the chapter. It is hoped that this format will allow you to identify the most important information in the chapter and make it easy to use the book again and again.

The book has been written so that it can be used by anyone who is involved in your organization's membership development efforts. Using the information in the book, you can put together a systematic and practical method for recruiting and keeping members. For the staff person responsible for membership, the book can be used as a constant source of ideas and suggestions. For the volunteer leaders who have committed to trying to help their organization grow, the book is designed to build confidence and serve as a resource base. For those who are new to the membership field it is a step-by-step description of what can be done and what should be done. And finally, for the more experienced membership person, it provides some new ideas and perhaps some new ways of implementing old ideas.

Chapter One:
Understanding The Importance of Membership

What to look for in this chapter:

- the ways that membership affects your organization's operations
- a test of your knowledge of your organization's membership function

Numbers are certainly an important part of the membership function, but you have to look way beyond the statistical aspects of membership to get a real appreciation for the impact that the membership function has on your organization. Membership growth is actually the *momentum* of your organization. When the membership function is working in your organization there will be a growing number of new members and steady or rising number of renewing members each year. This membership growth increases the **human resources** of the organization, works as a tool to recruit other new members and influence the organization's various publics, and has a dramatic effect on the organization's financial status.

Since most associations, societies, chambers of commerce, and other not-for-profit organizations have limited financial resources, they have to depend upon the volunteer work of their members to achieve the organization's goals. Without a steady stream of new people the group inevitably faces the problem of volunteer burnout. It is the new members joining this year who will become the leaders of the organization in the years to come.

People and companies want to be part of a successful organization. When your group continuously attracts and keeps members, it's a great **testimonial** to the value of membership. This concept of a growing organization is also important to many of the publics that your organization is trying to influence. These key publics include government officials, the media, standards-setting organizations, competing organizations, nonmembers, potential coalition partners, suppliers and vendors, and other institutions. At some point in an organization's relationship with each of these groups someone is going to ask how many members you have.

The **financial impact** of membership growth can't just be measured in terms of the dues dollars generated by members. It is always interesting to hear organizations say that they are not really dependent on membership since only a small percentage of their income comes from dues. That may be true, but just because an organization isn't dependent upon membership dues doesn't mean it isn't dependent upon membership. The people and companies who support your organization financially through insurance programs, conventions, educational functions and the like are in most cases your members. The amount of income they add to your organization through these other programs is certainly part of what has to be considered when calculating the value of membership to your organization.

Membership can also be one of the most rewarding and exciting jobs a person can have. Membership is one of the few jobs where every single day you know whether or not you're successful! In membership the measurements of your success are right in front of you all the time. If you have a plan and some skill and a lot of enthusiasm, you can look at those goals and truly take pride in achieving them.

Successful membership work can be a tremendous stepping stone in a professional staff person's career. To do well in membership development, you'll have to know everything that's going on in your organization. The more you know about your organization's programs, services, and benefits, the better you will be able to market them to potential members. The skills you can develop in the membership field include marketing, selling, oral and written communications, and others. These skills help you not only in membership work but also in other parts of your personal and professional life. Be glad that membership is one of your responsibilities and enjoy your work.

Be glad, too, that this book is available to help you be successful in membership. Enjoy the book, but most of all learn from it. Now it is time to get started.

BUT FIRST.......

Before you can start putting a membership development

program together to help your organization move forward, you need to be certain you know where you've been, where you are, and where you'd like to go.

Here's a short quiz for you to take. Follow along and fill in the answers as you read the questions. No fair looking up the answers!

1. How many total members are there in your organization right now? _____

2. How many members did your organization have one year ago? _____

3. How much money in your current year's budget is earmarked for membership recruitment? _____

4. How much money in your current year's budget is earmarked for membership retention? _____

5. Considering only your main membership category (i.e., "regular" or "voting" or "active"), what percentage of your potential members are already in? In other words, what is your market penetration? _____

6. What was your retention rate last year? _____ (Retention rate refers to the percentage of members who renewed their membership in your organization last year when compared to the total number of members you had at the end of the previous year.)

7. What will your retention rate be at the end of this year? _____

8. What does it cost your organization to recruit a new member? _____

9. What does it cost your organization to lose one member? _____

10. List your organization's three major competitors for members. _____

Now that wasn't so bad, or was it? This book will help you learn how to identify this information and use it to develop a plan of action for recruitment and retention. You can't just go out and start trying various recruitment and retention techniques without having a grasp on what you're trying to accomplish, what resources you have to work with, what your organization's history has been, what your cost of doing business is, and the other things covered in the quiz. If you couldn't answer some of the ten questions, go back and get the answers in the near future.

The opportunity is there. The challenges of membership have never been greater and neither have the rewards. After reading this book you'll feel more confident about your ability to help your organization grow.

Lessons learned:

- **membership provides the momentum for the rest of your organization's programs and services**
- **to be successful you'll need to know as much as possible about your organization's membership and history**
- **working in the membership area can help you develop skills you can use in other parts of your life**

Chapter Two:
The Membership Plan

What to look for in this chapter:
- the importance of a membership plan
- the key elements in a good plan
- a sample plan format that you can adapt to your organization

The first thing you need to do to assure success in membership development is to establish a plan of action. If there is no road map to guide staff members and the membership committee there can be a tendency to wander from one program to another hoping that something will work. If there is no definition of success, then how will you know when you have succeeded?

Having a membership plan is also important because it helps ensure some continuity in the membership function. If a two- or three-year membership plan can be established, then each year the people in charge of the membership function can be guided by the plan. Your organization's membership challenge then becomes determining which elements of the plan to implement each year in order to accomplish the established goals. This also assists your organization when there is a change in who is in charge of the membership function. Rather than having the new membership committee chair or staff person focus on some completely new aspect of membership, the plan allows these new people to take their creative energy and apply it to a specific part of your plan.

The overall goal of the membership function would seem to be obvious— try to recruit and retain as many members as possible. This really should be the membership goal, but you need to determine what is meant by "as many as possible" and whether or not there are there any limitations on how to get there. Membership goals and the strategies used to accomplish them should be part of a structured plan of action.

This chapter describes the major elements in a membership plan. These elements include the objective statements, the planning assumptions, the measurement criteria, the current measurements, goals for the future, and implementation strategies.

After a discussion of each element of the plan there is a sample of an actual plan that includes those elements. The sample plan has been provided by the California Farm Bureau Federation (CFBF), of Sacramento, California. CFBF used this plan to guide their efforts. The CFBF's plan as shown here is not the complete plan but an edited version so that only those parts which apply to the discussion in this chapter are shown.

The **objective statements** should briefly describe what the membership program is trying to accomplish. They should identify the general goals of each of the major areas of the membership development plan. When you write objective statements, use action words to tell what you are attempting to do in that area.

The California Farm Bureau Federation's objective statements included:

- *Reversing the recent decline in membership and having a net growth in membership within the first year of the plan.*

- *Raising the organization's retention rate each year for the next two years.*

- *Enhancing the CFBF's relationship with the county farm bureaus.*

These statements reflected the CFBF's objectives in the areas of total membership growth, membership retention and affiliate relationships. The tendency in many organizations would be to jump from these objective statements to a series of implementation strategies that would describe specific steps to take in each area to achieve the objective. However, if the membership plan is really going to guide your efforts, you need to take some intermediate steps before you start implementing any action strategies.

Before establishing how you are going to measure success and what your goals will be, you need to identify some **planning assumptions.** These assumptions are descriptions, projections or forecasts that your organization has made about what the conditions in your industry, community, or profession are expected to be over the period covered by your plan. Unless these assumptions are identified in your plan, there can be some doubt about the reasonableness of your goals and plan of action. Listing these assumptions also gives you a way to better monitor your progress in achieving your goals. If one or more of your original assumptions prove to be wrong you can go back and adjust your goals. For example, if you projected that the local economy in your chamber area was going to deteriorate and instead it improves dramatically, you might need to adjust your goals upward.

In the CFBF's case their assumptions included:
- There will be a continued shrinkage in the number of people farming, meaning fewer potential voting members.
- There will continue to be a growth in agriculture-related services and products, meaning a steady base of potential associate members.
- The farm economy in California will continue to improve.

After the objective statements are finalized and you have listed the assumptions you are making in putting your plan together, you need to identify **measurement criteria** for each objective. This is the part of the membership plan that people don't like because it involves identifying how your success is measured. And, it follows, if success is measurable, someone will be held accountable. That's what a good plan is supposed to do.

There can be more than one way to measure success in each objective area. It is important to prioritize these measurement criteria so that the people responsible for membership know how to allocate their resources. Here is how these measurement criteria elements of the CFBF membership plan looked.

Objective: *Reverse declining membership and achieve net growth within 1 year*
Measurement criteria (in priority order):
1. Total members at year-end compared to total members one year earlier
2. Number of new members recruited

This indicates that the CFBF's top priority measurement criterion is to grow, with any combination of new and renewed members. Once that is achieved they will measure how much of that growth was attributable to new member recruitment.

Objective: *Raise retention rate each year.*
Measurement Criteria (in priority order):
1. Overall retention rate in all categories compared to previous year
2. Retention rate of associate members compared to previous year

In this instance the CFBF is saying that raising their overall retention rate is the most important item. After that, they are going to concentrate on specifically increasing the retention rate among their associate members. This means that they will consider themselves successful in this part of the plan if their total retention rate goes up at all. They will consider themselves to be exceptionally successful if, within that total growth, associate member retention also goes up.

Objective: *Enhancing relationships with county farm bureaus*
Measurement criteria:
1. Number of county farm bureaus enrolled in membership campaign
2. Number of county farm bureau membership chairs attending campaign kickoff meeting

Since the CFBF depends on its county farm bureaus to do a lot of the recruiting, it sets specific measurement criteria in two areas of membership development that are shared opportunities between itself and the county organizations.

Your organization's entire plan of action could change depending upon the priorities and type of organization you have. For example, if one of your objectives is to generate additional dues income and your organization has a dues structure that has various categories, then your membership plan might include a targeted recruitment effort toward members in the larger dues categories. If all members pay the same dues, the recruitment efforts should be designed to simply get as many new members as possible. Each of these priorities would necessitate a different marketing plan. That's why it's so important that your organization's leadership establish priorities during each element of the membership plan.

After establishing the measurement criteria and prioritizing them, the **current measurement** of each criterion should be identified. This assures that goals are set in a reasonable manner and that everyone agrees on what the starting point was for measuring success. In the CFBF example the current measurements included:

Objective: *Reverse declining membership and achieve net growth within one year.*
Measurement criteria (in priority order):
1. Total members at year end compared to one year earlier
   Current measurement: 82,897 members
2. Number of new members recruited
   Current measurement: 9,834 new members last year

Objective: *Raise retention rate each year.*
Measurement Criteria (in priority order)
1. Overall retention rate in all categories compared to previous year
   Current measurement: 86% renewal rate last year
2. Retention rate of associate members compared to previous year
   Current measurement: 81% renewal rate last year

Objective: *Enhancing relationships with county farm bureaus.*
Measurement criteria:
1. Number of county farm bureaus enrolled in membership campaign
   Current measurement: 72 last year
2. Number of county farm bureau membership chairs attending campaign kickoff meeting
   Current measurement: 51 last year

Now that your current measurements are identified, **goals for the future** can be established. Membership goals should be based on more than wishful thinking or financial need. They should be based on reasonable projections, information provided by the staff and volunteer leaders, some sense of historical performance, and any statistical data available from the industry, community, or profession. The goals should be measurable, achievable, challenging, and clearly defined.

As we continue to follow the CFBF plan these goals for the future include:

Objective: *Reverse declining membership and achieve net growth within one year.*

Measurement criteria (in priority order):

1. Total members at year end compared to one year earlier
   Current measurement: 82,897 members
   Future goals: Year 1: 83, 500 members
                   Year 2: 87,000 members

2. Number of new members recruited
   Current measurement: 9,834 new members last year
   Future goals: Year 1:10,500 new members
                   Year 2:11,000 new members

Objective: *Raise retention rate each year.*

Measurement Criteria (in priority order):

1. Overall retention rate in all categories compared to previous year
   Current measurement: 86% renewal rate last year
   Future goals: Year 1: 87% renewal rate
                   Year 2: 88% renewal rate

2. Retention rate of associate members compared to previous year
   Current measurement: 81% renewal rate last year
   Future goals: Year 1: 82% renewal rate
                   Year 2: 83% renewal rate

Objective: *Enhancing relationships with county farm bureaus*

Measurement criteria (in priority order):

1. Number of county farm bureaus enrolled in membership campaign
   Current measurement: 72 last year
   Future goals: Year 1: 75 enrolled
                   Year 2: 83 enrolled

2. Number of county farm bureau membership chairs attending campaign kickoff meeting
   Current measurement: 51 last year
   Future goals: Year 1: 60 in attendance
                   Year 2: 65 in attendance

Once your organization knows what it's objectives are, what assumptions are being made about the future, how success will be measured, what the current measurements are, and what the goals for the future are, then you can begin identifying your **implementation strategies.** These strategies should be specific programs or activities designed to accomplish the membership objectives and should have some direct correlation to the measurement criteria.

Implementation strategies normally fall into two main categories: continuing programs and new programs. In the continuing program category, the plan should identify what membership activities your organization currently has and what improvements or changes will be made to those activities. Implementation strategies should also include at least one or two new activities the organization will initiate. Here is what the CFBF plan looks like after adding this final element of the plan.

Objective: *Reverse declining membership and achieve net growth within one year*

Measurement criteria (in priority order):

1. Total members at year-end compared to one year earlier
   Current measurement: 82,897 members
   Future goals: Year 1: 83, 500 members
                   Year 2: 87,000 members
   Implementation Strategies:
   Continuing programs: Recruitment letters, renewal invoicing system
   New programs: Booths at county fairs, county executives incentives
2. Number of new members recruited
   Current measurement: 9,834 new members last year
   Future goals: Year 1:10,500 new members
                   Year 2:11, 000 new members
   Implementation Strategies:
   Continuing programs: Telemarketing, membership campaigns
   New programs: Advertising campaign, trial memberships

Objective: *Raise retention rate each year.*
Measurement Criteria (in priority order):
1. Overall retention rate in all categories compared to previous year
   Current measurement: 86% renewal rate last year
   Future goals: Year 1: 87% renewal rate
                   Year 2: 88% renewal rate
   Implementation strategies:
   Continuing programs: Welcome packets, pre-invoice letters
   New programs: Early renewal incentive, personal calls from board members
2. Retention rate of associate members compared to previous year
   Current measurement: 81% renewal rate last year
   Future goals: Year 1: 82% renewal rate
                   Year 2: 83% renewal rate
   Implementation strategies:
   Continuing programs: Lower ad rates, mentor program
   New programs: Special recognitions in newsletter, reduced dues

Objective: *Enhancing relationships with county farm bureaus*
Measurement criteria:
1. Number of county farm bureaus enrolled in membership campaign
   Current measurement: 72 last year
   Future goals: Year 1: 75 enrolled
                   Year 2: 83 enrolled
   Continuing programs: Contests, incentive program
   New programs: Set own goals, competition by size of bureau
2. Number of county farm bureau membership chairs attending campaign kickoff meeting
   Current measurement: 51 last year
   Future goals: Year 1:60 in attendance
                   Year 2: 65 in attendance
   Continuing programs: Direct mail, testimonials
   New programs: Buddy system, board responsibility

Once the implementation strategies are identified they need to be **assigned** to an individual or group. This could be either the membership director, the membership committee, or both. A time frame for completing the implementation steps should also be established. Your detailed implementation plan should be written out, adopted officially by your organization's leadership, and communicated to everyone involved with the membership function in your organization.

By using a comprehensive and thoughtful membership plan your organization can use its limited resources in the most productive way. Just by going through the process of establishing a membership plan you will help your organization focus on the importance of the membership function. Perhaps most importantly, the plan helps to define success and gets members and staff committed to accomplishing the objectives and being successful as individuals and as a team.

Lessons learned:

- *a good membership plan can help define success*

- *the key elements of a good plan are objective statements, planning assumptions, measurement criteria, current measurements, implementation strategies, and assignment of responsibilities*

- *the membership plan will help keep your membership efforts focused*

Chapter Three:
Organizing for Success

What to look for in this chapter:
- *the role of the membership director in managing the membership function in your organization*
- *how the membership committee can be structured to help your efforts*

The success of your organization's membership efforts depends on three important factors. These factors include having a viable membership plan, having a capable membership director or other staff person, and having an effective membership committee of volunteer members.

In this chapter there is a discussion of the role of the membership director. There is also a description of how to develop an effective volunteer work force through your organization's membership committee.

The Membership Director

The **membership director** is the staff person in your organization with the greatest direct responsibility for membership recruitment and retention. This person is assigned to make certain that your organization accomplishes its membership goals in the most effective way. The membership director is truly the manager of the membership function.

Not every organization has the luxury of having a staff person who is assigned to do nothing other than membership work. If your organization has a staff of any size, someone needs to have the specific assignment of managing the membership operations.

Regardless of who fulfills the role of the membership director in your organization, there are several functions that should be performed. These functions include recruitment, retention, administration, research, motivation, follow-up work, chapter relations and leading by example.

Your organization has to decide if it expects the staff to actually **recruit members**. In some organizations the staff is expected to recruit even though staff members lack some of the credibility that members have as peers in the community, trade, or profession. The important thing is to find out at the beginning of the year what the expectations of the membership director are so he or she can allocate resources and manage his or her time effectively.

The membership director has a great deal to do with whether or not a member comes back for another year. **Retention** is a direct responsibility of the staff person because he or she has more day-to-day contact with the members than almost anyone in your organization. The membership director should be one of the reasons that members want to renew.

Administration is one of the main responsibilities of the staff. In addition to keeping the numbers and records, the staff needs to coordinate the resources in the membership areas.

The membership director also has the responsibility of doing as much background **research** work as possible before asking the volunteers to get involved. This includes prospecting and qualifying, finding out what others are doing, and developing training materials.

Someone has to take the lead in getting the volunteer leaders and other staff members **motivated,** interested and excited about membership. That job falls to the membership director. This includes showing the other members of the staff the value of the membership function and getting volunteers to feel confident of their ability to recruit and retain members.

When your organization is successful in getting members involved in recruiting and retention there is often a lot of **follow-up** work left to be done. During a membership campaign the members see a lot of prospects, but not all of them will join. Of the ones who don't join there are several who are more interested than they were before. However, there is no one to contact them again because the members have already done as much as they are going to do. This becomes the membership director's job.

If your organization has a **chapter** structure, a large part of the burden of making that a positive relationship falls to the membership director. This includes smoothing over relationship problems and trying to make the chapters understand that being affiliated with your organization is another reason for members to join or stay.

Perhaps the most important function of the membership director is to **lead by example.** If other members and staff see the membership director as a believer, and an effective professional, they will strive to help and emulate him or her. The Membership Director has a reason to know more about the organization than almost anyone else on the staff and should use that knowledge to help others understand the value of membership.

The Membership Committee

The most traditional way to get members involved in the membership function is to ask them to be part of your organization's **membership committee.** The membership committee is important for all of the same reasons that membership in general is important to your organization. The committee has additional roles in helping your organization accomplish its goals. A membership committee is a group that is solely focused on membership, and serves as a forum for new ideas on ways to recruit and retain members. The membership committee provides a structured way to get input from members and a vehicle that can be used for delegating tasks.

It can be difficult to get people to volunteer for this particular committee. This is due to the time commitment that working on any committee entails and the fact that when people think of serving on the Membership Committee, they also think of having to sell memberships. Selling any product or service is difficult for some people. Another reason people are reluctant to serve on the membership committee is that there is a very specific measurement for success.

Since the effectiveness of the membership committee can have a big impact on the success of your membership efforts, you should spend a lot of time and effort putting a good committee together. To do that you'll need to appoint or recruit a strong chairperson, recruit a willing and capable committee, and give the committee members specific responsibilities,

The Membership Committee has a big responsibility so try to get a **strong chairperson** to head the committee. Don't select someone as committee chair just because he or she has the time or because no one else wants the job. Try to identify which of your members has the skills and characteristics to do the job most effectively and ask that person to serve.

Look for someone in your organization who is energetic, knowledgeable about both the organization and the profession, industry, or community, well-respected, willing and able to give the time needed to do the job, and a self-starter, successful in her or his own career. In addition to having these personal qualities, a good chairperson should possess some leadership skills that would help him or her be successful. Some of these leadership skills would be facilitation skills to run effective committee meetings, recruiting skills for getting new members and getting committee help, delegation skills, organizational skills, time management skills, and marketing skills.

Finding someone with all of these characteristics and skills is probably an impossible task. The trick is to find someone with as many of these as possible and then expand their capabilities by providing training in the remaining key areas. If you can get a good leader for your membership committee you'll be off to a good start.

Once the chairperson is selected, a **willing and capable committee** needs to be put into place. The appropriate number of people for the committee will depend upon your organization's needs and resources. In large national and international organizations with substantial staff support, the committee might meet only once or twice a year and their main functions might be focused on policymaking and information gathering. In smaller regional organizations, the membership committee may be responsible for virtually all of the membership functions including recruitment, retention, membership campaigns, new member orientation and policy making. Each type of membership committee has specialized needs and the make-up of the committee should be tailored to meet organizational needs.

Regardless of the size or scope of the committee it is important to **give committee members specific responsibilities** rather than just asking them to be members of a committee. When a business person or professional is asked to serve on a membership committee, the first thought he or she has is that in participating on this committee he or she will be tied up in countless meetings, be pestered by the chairperson to sell, sell, sell, and will never see friends or family again. This is because so many people have had bad experiences working on committees.

To overcome this reluctance to participate in membership committee activities, your organization needs to employ a little-used leadership technique called *thinking small.* Rather than asking a member to just serve on a membership committee, ask him or her to take on a very specific role in membership. The thinking small part of it comes from taking a look at all of the functions and jobs that a membership committee is responsible for and breaking these functions down into smaller jobs that are less time consuming. There are several specific jobs that could be assigned to individuals on a Membership Committee. These jobs include recruitment, retention, member involvement, prospect list management, new member welcoming and orientation, trade show membership booth coordination, and member recognition.

It is easier for some people to agree to serve on a membership committee that breaks down the committee roles because they know they will be doing something worthwhile yet will be focused and able to work toward specific goals for a specific purpose. It is also an easier way to share the workload of the committee. It provides a structure for the delegation of tasks for the membership chairperson and it gives both the volunteer leaders and the organization's staff a chance to help individual members and the committee be successful.

Your organization needs to use all of its resources effectively to accomplish its membership goals. The membership director and the membership committee are two of the most important resources. It is important for the membership director and the membership committee to work as a team if they are going to be successful.

Lessons learned:
- *the membership director has the main responsibility for your organization's success in membership*
- *the membership director's roles include recruitment, retention, motivation, administration, follow-up, chapter relations, and leading by example*
- *an effective membership committee can add greatly to your organization's ability to accomplish its membership goals*
- *be sure to give membership committee members specific assignments such as prospecting, retention, recruitment, new member orientation, and membership campaigns*

SAMPLE 3-A
A sample job description for a membership director.

Position: Manager, Membership Programs

Job Responsibilities: To develop and manage membership recruitment and retention programs, and chapter relations programs. To ensure that the customer service activities and special projects of the Membership Department are completed in an accurate, efficient, and timely manner. To be knowledgeable about the organizational structure, bylaws, policies, and procedures of the organization to ensure efficient and timely operations of the department.

General/administrative Responsibilities:
1. Supervise chapter and member support and promotional activities of the department.
2. Prepare Executive Director Report on membership to the Board
3. Update department job descriptions.
4. Prepare annual membership marketing plan.
5. Prepare and present membership department orientation for new Board.
6. Serve as staff liaison to the Membership Committee.

Member Services Responsibilities:
1. Coordinate production with the communications department of the annual Membership Directory.
2. Update and coordinate production of information materials sent to members including new members kits, membership cards, and Bylaws.
3. Identify and develop new affinity programs/services that meet member needs.
4. Coordinate promotion of existing services such as car rentals, credit cards, etc.

Membership Promotion Responsibilities:
1. Set membership growth goals and plan strategies to attain those goals utilizing mail campaigns, member-to-member programs, inquiry cards, and member referrals.

2. Coordinate production and provide input on the theme, design, color, copy, and layout of all promotional materials, including brochures, letters, applications, etc.
3. Determine target audiences and approve selection of prospect lists and card deck insertions.
4. Coordinate with promotions coordinator, mailing schedule and mail house services.
5. Monitor and analyze testing and tracking results of all promotion efforts.

Member Retention Responsibilities:
1. Set retention goals and develop and implement strategies to attain those goals such as leadership training, membership awareness programs, exit surveys, new member newsletters, on-time renewal incentives, new member surveys and chapter retention campaigns.
2. Update and coordinate production and distribution of renewal notices and pre-renewal letters.

SAMPLE 3-B

A sample job description for a membership committee chairperson.

Primary Responsibility: The Membership Chairperson is the volunteer coordinator of all membership recruitment and retention program activities.

Specific Responsibilities:
1. Establish the membership committee as a mechanism for accomplishing recruitment and retention activities within the organization.
2. Conduct at least four membership committee meetings per year.
3. Delegate recruitment and retention activities to committee members.
4. Motivate and follow-up with committee members.
5. Develop (with appropriate staff) an annual recruitment and retention plan.
6. Develop a timetable for implementing each phase of the plan.
7. Evaluate the results of recruitment and retention programs.
8. Notify headquarters on a routine basis of all recruitment and retention activities and results.
9. Review monthly membership reports.

Internal relationships: Required to have frequent contact with organizational officers, members, and membership committee members.

External Relationships: Should have frequent contact with prospective members and the Membership Department at organizational headquarters.

Position Qualifications:
1. Ability to develop innovative ideas for recruitment and retention activities.
2. Willing to take responsibility for membership growth.
3. Ability to write effective recruitment and retention letters.
4. Outgoing, personable, and enthusiastic.
5. Strong organizational skills.
6. Sufficient time to devote to membership committee activities.
7. Knowledge and understanding of the organization, its members, its mission, and its goals.

Chapter Four
Identifying the Benefits of Joining

What to look for in this chapter:
- *how to develop empathy for your prospective members*
- *how to determine the difference between features and benefits*
- *how to articulate member benefits to attract new members*

In this chapter you'll learn why it's really important to understand the benefits of each of your organization's activities and how to describe those benefits to your prospective members. Gaining an understanding of organizational benefits is a crucial first step in putting together an effective membership program. Here is another "quiz" to help start this discussion.

On a sheet of paper write the number of people or companies that are prospective members for your organization's main membership category. Also write down how much it costs to join your organization in that category. If you're in an organization that has a number of dues categories, you can write down an average dues level.

Now list five reasons why a person or company should give your chamber, association or society that much money to join. Don't put down single words, like education or conventions. Write complete statements — almost as though you were writing a membership brochure. Remember, you are doing this quiz on the honor system, so no fair looking at your membership literature. After you've listed these five reasons to join try saying them out loud to yourself or to someone else.

Now take a look at what you've put down. In most cases you will have listed many of the specific programs and services that your organization provides. You may have listed programs like lobbying services, publications, educational opportunities, insurance, and other programs. These are good descriptions of what are called organizational *features*. A feature is a description of what your organization does. Unfortunately, most prospective members don't care what your organization does.

When a prospect is presented a list of features he or she basically thinks about the list and says to himself or herself, "So what? So what if this group has a lobbyist in Washington, D.C. and at the state capitol? So what if they have three monthly publications? So what if they have an insurance program?" The fact that you have these programs is only important to prospective members if they can understand how that feature will help them.

In order to do this you need to employ "Levin's Law of Membership Recruitment and Retention:"

- PERSONALIZE
- CUSTOMIZE
- EMPATHIZE

This means that to really be able to recruit members for your organization you have to learn to **think like a prospect**, not like a membership recruiter. To be able to retain members you have to think like a user of your organization's programs and services, not like the producer of those programs and services.

The challenge to being successful in membership recruitment and retention is to turn your association, society or chamber *features* into association, society or chamber *benefits*. Prospects and members want to know if your organization has any idea who they are and what they face when they go to work each day. Your job is to get the prospects believing that you do know who they are. This is how you personalize. The prospects also needs to know that your organization knows what they do for a living. This is how you customize. Finally the prospects must believe that your organization can help them do their job more effectively. This is how you empathize.

If you can get prospects to believe that you know who they are and what they do and that you can provide *benefits* to help them, you will have a good chance of getting them to join and a good chance of keeping them as members. No list of *features* will convince them to join or stay.

Benefits of Joining Trade Associations and Chambers of Commerce

In trade associations and chambers of commerce, the membership is generally in the name of the member companies. The focus of your benefits messages should be on company benefits.

Remember you are not running a charity. People don't give your organization their money and then just sit back and let you do whatever you want with it. If companies want to give money to a charity, they have plenty of options other than your association or chamber. When a company joins a trade association or chamber, it's an investment — a business investment. When any business makes an investment, it expects a return on its investment in the form of increased profit.

In business there are really only two ways to make money. One way is by increasing sales and the other way is by reducing expenses. What companies really want from a trade association or chamber membership, in short, is **a competitive advantage.** They don't want a competitive advantage over just any company, but specifically over those companies that didn't pay the dues and join the association or chamber.

So don't just tell prospects what your organization does, tell prospects how what your organization does will help them make a profit and be more competitive.

Look back at your list of reasons to join your organization. Read them back to yourself and see if they really answer the "So what?" question that is going through your prospects' minds. If you feel your statements are not clear about the specific benefits that those programs and services provide, look through the following descriptions of some of the most frequently mentioned programs that trade associations and chambers of commerce offer. These descriptions should help you better focus your message.

Government Relations

Government relations is an important program that takes a lot of the association's or chamber's resources. It is also one of the first benefits mentioned to a prospect. The assumption is made that the prospect will understand how important a government relations program is. If you think like a prospect, however, when you hear an organization say that it will represent you in Washington, D.C., or at the state capitol, what you're really hearing is the feature of the program and not the benefit. To turn this feature into a benefit, you've got to present it from the prospect's point of view. That's how your organization shows empathy.

In a trade association or chamber of commerce, there are two distinct benefits of the government relations program. It *reduces the cost of doing business* by keeping government regulations and paperwork burden as well as specific anti-business laws from hurting your members' businesses. The other benefit of your organization's government relations efforts is that it works to *protect, and where appropriate expand, members' markets.* Doesn't that sound more like a benefit than just stating that you have a government relations program?

Networking Opportunities

There is no doubt that one of the membership benefits promoted most aggressively is the ability for members to meet with their peers to share ideas and information. This is often referred to as *networking opportunities.* Most organizations present this feature of membership by listing and describing the many functions held throughout the year. The assumption, again, is that the prospect understands the benefit of the networking feature.

However, if you are a prospective member, networking sounds like a feature that is going to require that you spend a lot of time attending meetings. When you think of it like that it's not such a great benefit. It becomes even less of a benefit when you inform the prospect that in order to attend many these great networking meetings they have to pay an additional fee. Now the prospect is really thinking, "So what?"

To convince a prospect that networking is a real benefit, you need to explain this aspect of membership from the potential member's perspective. Trade association and chamber meetings and conventions can do several things for the prospect's company. By bringing the industry together your organization gives members the chance to make contact with potential customers. The benefit here is that it helps increase sales. Meetings put members in touch with suppliers and thereby help to reduce costs. At these meetings, members learn from the speakers and attendees ways to better market their products and services and ways to reduce costs through better management of their business. This is an especially appealing benefit in bad economic times. If your organization sponsors a trade show, the benefit is the time and money you've saved members by bringing all of these new products and suppliers together at the same place and time.

Publications

If you mentioned publications in your list of reasons to join, take another look at your statement and see if the real benefit of that feature is clear. Trade associations and chambers often tell companies that if they join, they'll receive all of your publications including your monthly newsletter, your quarterly magazine, your weekly legislative updates and other communications. The prospects hear about all of these publications and begin to get the impression that when they join they'll be inundated with mail they won't have time to read any way. That's hardly a benefit of membership.

You need to tell the prospects that when they begin receiving your publications they'll be getting a steady stream of ideas and information that can help them manage their businesses more profitably through better marketing ideas, new product information and cost-reducing management tips. Now that's a benefit of joining.

Other Programs and Services

Trade associations and chambers of commerce also offer a variety of member benefit services and programs that include such things as insurance programs, credit card programs and car rental agreements. The obvious value of these programs is that they *reduce cost,* and indeed they should be promoted that way. The thing to keep in mind about these programs is that many of them are available to your members through other sources. When members join to receive one of these services and later find they can get it cheaper from another source, the membership is threatened. This makes it even more important for organizations which depend upon these programs to recruit members to have an effective retention program in place. Then if insurance rates go up, for example, members still feel there are reasons to stay.

Each of these examples shows not only that you understand members' needs but also that you have ways to help meet these needs. You need to make certain that all of your organization's membership marketing literature, letters, telemarketing programs and other recruitment methods are focused on the benefits to the prospect and not on the features of the association or chamber of commerce.

Benefits of Joining Professional Societies

With professional societies the focus of your membership recruitment efforts will be a little different. The membership is in the name of the individual and the reasons for joining are even more personalized. This doesn't mean that you don't have to be concerned about the prospects perceiving a return on their investment. Professional society membership is no more of a charity than trade association or chamber membership. Membership is still an investment - except that in this case, it's a *career* investment. You still need to display empathy by getting the prospects to believe that you know what their professional challenges are and that membership in your organization can help. When you describe your professional society's programs and services you still have to overcome the "So what?" attitude of prospects.

There are three basic benefits people seek when they join professional societies. They join for *peer recognition,* for *job opportunities* and *career advancement* , and for *continuing education.*

Peer recognition is an important benefit because people want to be recognized as leaders in their chosen field. In some cases, just being a member of your society is a form of recognition.

Job opportunities and career advancement are benefits that professional societies sometimes try, unnecessarily, to downplay. Promoting job opportunities as a reason to join doesn't necessarily mean that a person who is interested in switching employers will find another one through your organization, although that may well be the case. If the person becomes a more valued employee to a current employer through membership in your society, that certainly advances his or her career.

Continuing education is self-explanatory. In many professions continuing education is a requirement for continued practice. In all professions it will help lead to the other two important benefits, peer recognition and job opportunities.

Just as you do in trade associations and chambers, don't tell prospects the features of what your organization does, tell them how what your organization does can give them one of the three basic benefits of membership. Here are some suggestions for identifying benefits in professional societies.

Publications

Publications are without question a key benefit for professional society members. The fact that they exist isn't what's important. That's the "So what?" In professional societies, publications actually can provide all three benefits people seek. Your publications are one of your most basic forms of continuing education. Many articles are written by members, so there is a chance for peer recognition. In some instances the publications have listings of job openings which offer job opportunities and career advancement .

Networking

Meetings are an important part of professional societies, too. The benefits of attending these meetings need to be expressed in a way that convinces prospects that it's worth their time to attend. Rather than just saying that your organization offers several important networking opportunities, try to describe the real benefits of getting together at your group's meetings, conventions and educational programs. When people attend your professional society's functions they get to meet and work with the leaders in your field. That's a form of peer recognition. The speakers and topics at these meetings are another form of continuing education. There are opportunities to talk to potential employers and find out where there are job openings.

Government Relations

For many professional societies, the area of government relations or lobbying is not that important since they are not structured to participate in this type of activity. Your organization may even be prohibited from using members' dues for this purpose. If your society does perform lobbying and advocacy functions for your members, you still need to promote those programs in terms that are meaningful to prospects and members. In professional societies, the lobbying function is designed to do two things: protect the members' right to practice their profession, and help set the conditions and standards under which the members will practice. After establishing why your society is involved in government relations, you can then describe the specific legislative or regulatory issues you've addressed that support those objectives.

Professional societies must focus their marketing message on the benefits of joining from the prospect's point of view and not on the features of joining from the society's point of view. What your organization does is not what is important; what it does for the prospect's career is.

Turning Intangible Benefits Into Reasons to Join

In every trade association, professional society, and chamber of commerce, there are opportunities to attract members through what are sometimes called the *intangible benefits.* One such benefit is the ability to give something back to an industry or a profession or a community. Intangible benefits can be used to recruit members, especially in professional societies, where you can appeal to an individual's commitment to a profession. This makes the membership even more personal. In trade associations you are trying to appeal to a corporate attitude or sense of social responsibility, which can be more difficult. Chambers of commerce also have some opportunities to appeal to a businessperson's sense of community spirit and support. In all organizations, there are certainly people and companies that will join organizations because they believe it's the right thing to do.

You need to be careful about trying to use intangible benefits as the focus for your recruitment efforts. There aren't that many prospects who will join just because they believe in your organization's goals and principles. In most industries, professions, and communities, these believers are already in! With few exceptions you are trying to recruit *non-believers*. In order to get these people and companies to join, you've got to show them the specific, usable, tangible benefits of membership. After you've convinced them of the tangible benefits of joining, you can add the intangibles to your list. Now you have a great benefits' package.

Lessons learned

- *focus your recruitment efforts on the benefits of joining, not on the features of what your organization does*

- *try to think like a prospect when identifying membership benefits*

- *trade associations and chambers of commerce offer prospective members the chance to gain a competitive advantage through the benefits of increased sales and reduced costs*

- *professional societies offer prospective members the chance to enhance their careers through peer recognition, job opportunities, and continuing education*

- *the three keys to effective membership recruitment and retention are the ability to personalize your message, the ability to customize your approach, and the ability to empathize with the prospect*

SAMPLE 4-A

This is a sample of how one professional society's membership brochure describes the benefits of joining. Note that although they only highlight three reasons to join (continuing education, job opportunities, and peer recognition), they list many programs and services that support those three benefits.

 Public Relations Society of America

WHAT CAN PRSA MEMBERSHIP DO FOR YOU?

IT'S AS SIMPLE AS 1... 2... 3...

1. PRSA CAN HELP YOU GET AHEAD IN YOUR CAREER

through its Information Center, a collection of information resources that includes custom research, the profession's Body of Knowledge, case histories, abstracts, manuscripts, books and on-line research services. In any profession, information and advancement go hand-in-hand.

through its career placement services, a job hot line of recorded, up-to-date service available 24 hours a day, featuring geographic locations, salary ranges and experience required. Soon to be available, *Public Relations Opportunities* newsletter, full of current position openings just for public relations professionals. The *Career Search Information Kit* contains everything you need to succeed in your search. When you <u>do</u> need to find that new position, PRSA is there for you.

through its Annual Conferences and meetings, where you'll meet, and learn from, the leaders in the field. To be a success, study the "masters" - with PRSA's help.

2. PRSA CAN PROVIDE VIRTUALLY ALL OF YOUR CONTINUING EDUCATION NEEDS

through its publications, which bring the latest in opinions, trends, and in-depth, practical information right to your doorstep. *Public Relations Journal, Public Relations TACTICS* (PRSA's new, monthly newspaper) and the *Register* (PRSA's membership directory), are all part of your membership package - convenient, concise and indispensable.

through Professional Development Seminars, Professional Interest Sections and chapter workshops, that allow you to set your own course, and be a part of the profession right where you live and work. Chapters meet regularly to help members overcome real-life problems with real-life solutions.

through Home Study Courses, a video library, and audio training sessions, that let you develop a customized program to meet everyone's needs – yours, your employer's (through in-company training), and your clients'. With topics like research, crisis management and media relations, you *know* that PRSA understands what it takes to succeed, and these educational aids are designed to help you do just that.

3. PRSA CAN GIVE YOU THE RECOGNITION YOU WANT – AND DESERVE

through the setting of professional standards that require all PRSA members to practice their profession at the highest levels of efficiency and integrity. The words "PRSA Member" on your letterhead and business card tell your clients – and your peers – that they're working with someone who is committed to delivering only the best!

through professional Accreditation, providing the ultimate symbol of achievement and competence, the APR (Accredited in Public Relations) designation. Earning the APR gives you the unique distinction of being officially recognized as a leader in your chosen profession.

through the industry's most prestigious award series, which honors the finest public relations programs with the Silver Anvils (the "Oscars" of the profession), program tactics with the Bronze Anvils, and individual achievement through the Gold Anvil, the Lund Public Service Award and the Outstanding Educator Award. The top professionals have earned the top recognition - and PRSA makes sure they get it!

SAMPLE 4-B
This chamber of commerce presented its benefits in the form of a resume. The message to the prospect is that you really don't join the chamber, you <u>hire</u> the chamber to help your business.

We want to work for you!   Check our resume!

CAPITAL REGION
Chamber of Commerce

Address: 114 Walnut Street, P.O. Box 969, Harrisburg, PA 17108-0969
Phone: (717) 232-4121

Objective: To share common business interests and experiences in pursuit of collective goals, to provide strength and organizational solidarity within the business community, to lobby effectively at all levels of government, to implement and execute visionary projects, and to present members with exceptional opportunities to network on behalf of themselves and their business interests.

Professional Experience: Over the past number of years, in excess of 180 new projects amounting to more than $278,000,000 in growth and over 10,000 new jobs have resulted through the direct and indirect activities of the Chamber and affiliated organizations. Membership with the Capital Region Chamber of Commerce is a VALUABLE investment:

*	V	Voice in legislation through Government Affairs Department
*	A	Affiliate programs such as Leadership Harrisburg Area
*	L	Leadership through committee involvement
*	U	Unity to pursue collective goals
*	A	Active role in community development
*	B	Business reputability and referrals
*	L	Local networking opportunities are numerous
*	E	Employee development and education through seminars

Assets: Approximately 1,500 members with more than 3,500 representatives united to make the Capital Region one of the strongest business communities in Pennsylvania; sixteen committees commited to lobbying for, informing, recruiting, awarding and retaining members; INSIGHTS, the monthly newsletter; and direct member benefits including Group 5 Health Insurance from Blue Cross/Blue Shield.

References: United States Chamber of Commerce Accreditation
Pennsylvania State Chamber of Business and Industry
Capital Region Economic Development Corporation
The City of Harrisburg
Mechanicsburg Naval Ships Parts Control Center
Hershey Entertainment & Resort Corporation
Harrisburg International Airport
Harrisburg Hilton and Towers

SAMPLE 4-C
This trade association also used the method of listing the main benefits of joining in a general sense (reducing costs and increasing sales) and then showed how various organizational programs and services supported those benefits.

Bottom-line Profits
to Save You Money!
You can't afford not to join . . .

❏ **Get Immediate Returns on Your Investment!**

* Reduced rates on MasterCard and Visa with Elan Financial Services and Discover.

* Commissions and volume discounts with Sprint operator services.

* Increased savings on Workman's Comp and bigger dividends on liability insurance with Threshermen's Insurance.

❏ **Increase Your Sales!**

* Receive a free listing in WIA's travel guide, "Where To Stay In Wisconsin!" Over 300,000 copies are distributed annually.

❏ **Lower Your Overhead!**

* Get answers to your many varied questions by calling WIA's full-time, professional staff. Save the cost of many phone calls.

* Lower your employee turnover rate through attendance at WIA seminars and workshops - trained employees are satisfied employees.

* Use WIA's legal assistance for help in collecting unpaid guest charges - or get answers to your legal questions.

* Proaction and reaction to legislation by WIA's legislative consultant saves innkeepers money by strengthening the business climate.

❏ **Get the Edge on Your Competition!**

* Hear about new ideas to make your operation more cost effective in each monthly issue of *Inn Touch*. This publication will help you keep up on current information about the industry.

* Attend WIA's Annual Convention and Trade Show - hear professional speakers, share ideas, learn about new products and services available to you.

❏ **Belong for Your Own Good!**

A SAMPLING OF ADDITIONAL BENEFITS:
* National Affiliation
* Wisconsin Lodging Law Book
* Weatherproof Inherent Risk Signs
* Career's Day Presentation packets
* Special Discount Coupons
* Co-op Advertising Opportunities
* Committee Involvement
* Recognize your employees with an Affiliate membership

CHAPTER FIVE

IDENTIFYING and QUALIFYING PROSPECTS

What to look for in this chapter:
- *how to identify the best sources for names of prospective members*
- *what additional information you need to make better use of the names*
- *how to match your knowledge of the prospects to specific benefits*

Having a wonderful set of easily identifiable benefits is only the first step in recruitment. A good message aimed at the wrong market is about as effective as giving a great speech to an audience that doesn't speak your language.

The next step in successful membership recruitment is making certain that you are talking to the right people. One of the biggest mistakes organizations make in their membership efforts is not doing a good job of identifying and qualifying prospective members. Qualifying prospects means learning more about the prospects than just their names and addresses and then using what you know to customize and personalize your solicitations to these members.

Among the sources you can use to identify prospective members are referrals, nonmembers who participate in your organization's programs, unsolicited inquiries, former members, and purchased lists. Your knowledge of each of these sources of names can assist you in your efforts to customize and personalize your recruitment efforts.

Referrals

Referrals are names of potential prospects given to you by your members or people who are affiliated with your organization. Referrals are usually among the very best prospects an organization has because of their direct connection to someone or some company that is already a member. You can get referrals from members by sending a referral card to members and asking them to send back the names of prospective members, by putting an article in your newsletter with a reply card or a phone number to call for more information, by having referral forms available at your meetings and educational programs, and by asking members of your board, committees, and other leadership groups to take time out of their meetings to give you some names.

These are all voluntary referral methods. If your organization is having trouble getting members to respond to these requests for names of prospects, it may be due to the fact that the requests are done too frequently and members just run out of ideas of who to refer. There may also be a reluctance to identify prospects because the member feels it would be intrusive to do so. To overcome this difficulty in getting names of prospects from your members, you can offer an incentive to members to send names of prospects to you. This incentive could be a free publication or a small recognition item such as a lapel pin. If the prospect who is referred eventually joins the member could get an additional reward. The additional incentive serves to encourage the member not only to send in a name but also to get involved in actually trying to get the prospect to join.

One way to overcome the possibility that members will run out of ideas on who to refer is through a *timed prospecting drill*. This entails taking a short amount of time out of one of your board or membership committee meetings to write down the names of every company with whom they've done business in the last three months, or the names of all the new people in their department, or the names of all the new businesses that have started in their area. This differs from just asking for names of prospects because it doesn't require the member to do any thinking about whether or not a person or firm is a "good" prospect. Once you compile this list, you can eliminate those who are already members. The remaining names are usually good prospects because you know something more about them than just their names. You also know who among your current members might be able to help you get the prospect to join.

When you do get a list of referrals, be sure to use whatever information you have gained about them to customize your approach. Don't just take these referrals and add them to your list of prospects to whom you plan to send your standard prospect packet. If you do this you've lost the considerable advantage of having received that name from a current member. When writing to a prospect who has been referred by a current member, you should mention in the very first sentence or paragraph that you're writing at the suggestion of that specific member. This is part of the process of customizing your recruitment efforts. Mentioning the name of the member who made the referral is also important when making telephone or personal contacts.

Most organizations are pretty good about using referrals appropriately by mentioning the name of the referring member. What many organizations do not do frequently enough is tell the member who gave the referral what they did with the referral. If you don't inform the person giving you a referral what follow-up action you took, there is no incentive for that person to give you any more names. Furthermore, there is certainly no incentive for the member to get involved in helping to do the actual recruiting.

If you send a follow-up letter to the prospect, send a copy to the person who referred the prospect. It would be even more effective to add a handwritten note to the copy of the letter sent to the referring member telling her or him that this letter has been sent and encouraging the member to make a follow-up call to the prospect. The member may or may not take the extra step and make the call; but, if you don't ask, the call will most certainly not be made.

Nonmembers Who Use Your Organization's Services

A second method of identifying prospects is by tracking the activities of what are called **nonmember users.** This term refers to nonmembers who attend your meetings and educational programs, buy your publications and otherwise participate in your organization's programs and services without actually joining. These non-member users should be excellent prospects because they have already expressed some obvious interest in something your organization has to offer. Don't lose the advantage of knowing something about these prospects by following up with them in the very same way you would follow up with someone who has never participated in one of your programs. You need to customize your follow-up with these prospects by making some reference to the specific program or service they've already used. This shows the prospects that you were paying attention when they participated. It also sends the prospects the message that this is the kind of personalized attention they can expect if they join. It also gives you an opportunity to "do a Jolson " on them. To "do a Jolson" means to tell the prospects that if they liked the program or service that they've already used, they're <u>really</u> going to like all of the other benefits they'll get if they join.

The term "do a Jolson" comes from a legend about Al Jolson, who was most famous for being the star of the first talking picture, *The Jazz Singer,* in 1927. Jolson was also one of the greatest singers and entertainers of the 1920s and 1930s and the legend was that he was also quite superstitious. Reportedly, Jolson would stay in the dressing room while waiting to perform and he would run the water in the sink so he wouldn't have to hear the applause for the act that appeared before he did. On one such occasion, Jolson was preceded on stage by none other than Enrico Caruso, who was perhaps the greatest opera tenor of all time. When Jolson was called on stage the audience was still cheering and shouting for Caruso, who had just given one of his best performances. This was the time when Jolson supposedly first uttered what was to become his trademark phrase. He finally got the audience settled down by screaming, "Hold it! Hold it! Hold it! You ain't heard *nothin'* yet!"

That's the message you want to get across to nonmember participants - what you've seen is nothing compared to what members get.

Finally, if it's at all possible within your organization's dues structure and policies, add a postscript at the end of your cover letter that lets the prospects know if they join in the next 30 days you'll credit the nonmember premium they paid to participate in any program toward their first-year dues. This gives the prospect an extra incentive to make the decision to join now.

Unsolicited Inquiries

Another source for adding to your prospect list is through **unsolicited inquiries.** When people or firms contact your organization and ask for membership information without any prior contact from you they are making an unsolicited inquiry. Obviously, something has attracted them to your organization. Knowing what that attraction is will make it easier for you to follow up on a personalized basis. Many times, however, all you have is a name, address and phone number so you really don't know much about them. To use these prospects effectively, it really takes a team effort.

This team effort is critical because the person in charge of membership isn't always the person who talks to the prospect. The basic request for membership information may have been taken by a receptionist, by a member of the education department, the meetings department, or some other department. Everyone in your organization should be able to help personalize the follow-up with the prospect by getting something more than just basic information. This doesn't mean that everyone should try to recruit the caller over the phone because that would be extremely difficult to organize. Everyone can help by just asking one or two questions of the caller before hanging up. This small but important step can make a big difference. If the only information obtained is a name and address, you have nothing to help you customize or personalize your follow-up. If the person taking the call can also find out how long the person has been in the field or how many employees his or her company has, then the person doing the follow-up can begin that follow-up in a very different and focused manner.

One way to help make this system work in your organization is to develop a form that all staff members can keep on their desks. The form should list the two or three basic questions to ask whenever anyone talks to a nonmember.

Former Members

Another source of prospects that has a lot of potential, as well as some hidden dangers, is your list of **former members.** These are people who have been in your organization in the past and for one reason or another have dropped out. Some people consider former members to be excellent prospects because they know about the organization, they've already made the decision to join at least once, and they have some sense of commitment to their industry, community, or profession. Other people consider former members to be bad prospects because they believe that there must be some type of negative feeling about your organization and some specific reasons why they dropped out.

If you are going to convince former members to rejoin your organization, you need to approach them in a special and personalized way. The first thing to do is to check your organization's membership prospect files and remove all of your former members from that current prospect file. Put your former members in a separate database file and develop a completely different recruitment campaign for these prospects. You cannot approach former members the same way you approach people or companies that have never been members. If former members get a letter or phone call to introduce them to your organization, they are going to think that you don't know who they are. They are also going to think that they have heard all this before and were disappointed. This will make it even harder to get the former member's attention.

Before you approach former members about rejoining the organization there are two things you'll really need to know. The most important thing to know is why they left. This isn't always possible to ascertain; however, if you can find out why they left, enter that information somewhere in your records. That will enable you to understand something about the person's mindset and gives you an opportunity to overcome that mindset in your correspondence or personal contacts.

The other thing you'd like to know about former members is when they left. Knowing how long a former member has been out can actually help you focus on ways to convince them to rejoin.

The reason these two factors are important is because when you approach a former member about rejoining your organization you really only have to answer one question. That question is "What's new?" You need to tell them what has happened since they left the organization that makes it meaningful for them to join again right now.

Former members are special people. You need to make it clear you know they used to be members and there is a reason for them to come back at this particular time. Your basic message should tell them that a lot has changed since they were members and they need to take another look at your organization now. Knowing how long it has been since they were last members helps you determine which new things to emphasize.

Purchased Lists

Another way to develop a good list of prospects is through **mailing lists** that you can purchase from private firms or obtain from public sources. Purchased lists are a necessity in many organizations because you have so many prospects that it is impractical to maintain all of the pertinent information internally. In some professions and industries there are minimum legal or licensing requirements to practice or to operate a business, so reliable sources of prospect lists in these areas are available through the agency or organization that oversees the licensing or awarding of credentials.

If you are purchasing mailing lists from vendors or agencies there are several things you can do to improve the chances that you are working from a good list. Try to find out what sources of information are being used in compiling these lists. Be sure these sources are credible for your purposes. When you are buying mailing lists try to find out how often the vendor updates the lists. Ask what the date of the last update was so you can get the most recent lists. You also want to find out whether or not you can get discounts if you are going to be purchasing multiple copies. Many vendors who sell mailing lists to associations and chambers are willing to negotiate their rates if you are willing to be a consistent customer of theirs.

Find out what demographic breakouts the list supplier can provide. If you don't specify what you want in a list you'll get only the basic information. The list supplier may very well be able to give you additional information such as a breakdown of companies with a certain amount of employees or of individuals with a certain amount of experience in the field. Each additional piece of demographic information helps you customize your approach.

Other Membership Organizations

The member rosters of **other associations, societies or business groups** can also be a source of potential members for your organization. The fact that a company or an individual has joined another organization is a good sign because you know that he or she understands the value of being part of an organization. So, you won't have to sell them on that concept. On the other hand, they've already made a commitment to that organization so they have a built-in loyalty to that group. When you approach prospects who are members of other organizations you need to be certain that you know your competition. Knowing your competition allows you to customize and personalize your approach by focusing on the benefits your organization can provide that other organizations can't.

Further Qualifying Your Prospect Lists

You now have many potential sources for creating your prospect list. The fact of the matter is that most organizations really don't have any trouble identifying potential members. If you carefully review the list of sources — referrals from current members, unsolicited inquiries, nonmember users, former members, purchased lists, and other organizations — you'll find that all of the names of the people or organizations on these lists makes up most of the prospects that are *eligible* to join your organization. If you have unlimited resources, having a list of all of the people or companies that are eligible to join is fine. Unfortunately most organizations don't have unlimited resources. Therefore, after you've created your list you need to identify which individuals or companies are most *likely* to join. To determine who is most likely to join you have to further qualify your prospects.

Qualifying prospects means gaining more information about them than just their names and addresses. As you add to your information base about each prospect or group of prospects you are also adding to your ability to match your organization's benefits to the specific needs of those members. This is an important step in personalizing and customizing your recruitment efforts.

In trade associations and chambers of commerce where most

members are corporations or businesses, you should try to obtain as much information about the company as possible before approaching that company about joining. Some of the things you'd like to know about these companies would include what size they are (in terms of sales or number of employees), who is the ultimate decision maker in the company, whether or not the company specializes in a particular product or service, and what other organizational affiliations they have.

Knowing the size of the prospective member company is important for two reasons. First of all, if you know the size of a company, then you may be able to identify specific programs or services that can help a company of that size. For example, larger companies may be interested in some of your information or educational programs on work force management or labor relations. A smaller company may be interested in information about running a family-owned business. When you approach prospects, approach them with the knowledge that you've got specific programs to help their particular needs. You can only do that if you've done some additional qualifying beyond determining that they are eligible to join.

The second reason why knowing the size of a company is important is that in some organizations the dues structure is based on the size of the company. When you approach prospects knowing how big they are, you will also know how much money it is going to cost them to join your organization. You can assume that sometime during the course of the solicitation of the prospects, the cost of membership is going to come up. By knowing their size you can be prepared to discuss the benefits of joining at that particular dues level.

Identifying the ultimate decision maker in a prospective member company is important because that is the person you want to have involved in the actual discussion about joining your organization. It can be a wasted effort to convince someone to join only to have them tell you that they still have to get it approved by someone else. This means you are now relying on someone else to communicate your benefits message to the decision maker.

You also want to know if a company has any kind of specialty. Some companies specialize in a particular part of the marketplace. If you know what that specialty is you can customize your approach.

One final thing you should find out is what other organizational affiliations this company has. By talking to others and doing additional research, try to determine if the prospective member company is a member of one of your competing organizations or of other general or specialty business organizations. If you know that the company is a member of other groups, you can focus your approach by concentrating on the benefits your organization offers that the others don't. You also can eliminate any general discussion about the value of business organizations because this company obviously already understands the value of joining a group. Your job is to convince them to join yours, too.

Qualifying prospects for membership in **professional societies** is a slightly different task. Some of the things you'd like to know about individuals who are prospects for professional societies include their educational background, how long they have been in the profession, for whom they work, and their other professional affiliations.

Since continuing education is one of the most important reasons for joining a professional society, knowing a person's educational level allows you to highlight those parts of your educational programs that are consistent with the educational level or needs of the potential member. The benefit you are trying to highlight is the ability for continuing education to help the person move on to the next level in the profession.

How long the prospect has been in the profession is important because some organizations have programs for new practitioners or people just entering the field out of school. Other organizations have programs that are specifically for people who are nearing the end of their career. Some even have retired member categories.

Many companies and organizations have a tradition of encouraging their employees to join professional societies and organizations. If you know that an individual works for one of those employers, you have an opportunity to customize your approach. If you can also find out if this employer has a tradition of paying the individual's dues, then that fact will help you customize your approach even more. When the employer is paying, you have to convince the prospect to find the money in a particular budget. If the prospective member is going to have to pay the dues out of his or her own personal funds then you have to personalize the approach even more.

As is the case in a trade association or chamber of commerce, you'd also like to know if prospects are members of other professional societies. This knowledge can help you identify specific benefits that they are not already receiving and concentrate on the <u>new</u> benefits membership in your organization offers.

Lessons Learned in This Chapter

- *among the best sources of names of prospective members for your organization are referrals from current members, non-members who use your organization's services, unsolicited inquiries, former members, purchased lists, and the rosters of other organizations*

- *use your knowledge of the source of the names to customize and personalize your approach to them*

- *do additional research on your prospects to further qualify them as those who are likely to join and not just those who are eligible to join*

SAMPLE 5-A

This is a chart developed by a professional society to pinpoint which of their main benefits would have the most appeal to specific target markets. They used this chart to develop their membership literature and cover letters. They listed all of their benefits but highlighted the ones that had been identified as most valuable for each target group.

MARKET SEGMENT	QUALIFIER 1 Self-employed	QUALIFIER 2 Corporate Setting	QUALIFIER 3 Former Member
NEW TO THE PROFESSION	Benefits insurance cont.education networking	Benefits job opportunities cont.education recognition	Benefits not applicable
MID-CAREER	Benefits cont.education practice protect.	Benefits other members technology	Benefits changes
SENIOR LEVEL	Benefits recognition legislation	Benefits recognition man. education legislation	Benefits changes recognition

SAMPLE 5-B

This is a list of some sources of potential members for organizations. After looking at each source you should try to determine if this source applies to your organization, and how to use the information about where the name came from in your follow-up efforts.

The list at the bottom is a sample listing of the information about a prospect you might want to have before approaching him or her about joining your organization.

Sources of Names

Source   Applicable (Y/N)   How to Use

Referrals (from current members)
Inquires (cold)
Nonmember "users"
Former Members
Purchased Lists
Trade Directories
Yellow Pages
Other Associations
Licensing/Accrediting Agencies

Things you'd like to know about a prospect if you could

Trade Associations and Chambers (Corporate Memberships)	Professional Societies (Individual Memberships)
Size/# employees/volume	Age
Need	Education
Former member?	Former member?
Decision maker	Other affiliations
Specialty	Employer
Association Contacts	Length of time in profession
Reputation	Will employer pay dues?
Other Affiliations	

Chapter SIX
Overcoming Objections

What to look for in this chapter:
- *the most common objections to joining an organization*
- *the importance of anticipating objections and being prepared*
- *suggestions for overcoming the most common objections*

Even when organizations have a good benefits message that is presented effectively to qualified prospects, there will be some people or companies that still won't join right away. Anticipating and overcoming objections effectively is a skill that membership volunteers and staff members need to master if they are going to really maximize their membership efforts. An objection is simply a statement made or question asked by a prospect that expresses reluctance to join the organization. In this chapter there is a discussion of the most frequently given objections and suggestions on how to overcome them.

One thing to keep in mind is that if your organization is using direct mail as its major method of recruiting new members, there will be no one to answer these questions or objections for the prospects. The only option is to address and overcome objections directly in the literature. That can be difficult because it is impossible to determine which prospects have which objections. This is where techniques like telemarketing and one-on-one recruiting provide opportunities that aren't available with direct mail. Telemarketing and one-on-one recruiting allow you to listen to specific objections and respond with specific answers.

Regardless of which recruiting method is used, prospective members will have objections. The most important thing to remember when thinking about ways to overcome objections is to *listen carefully* to what the prospect is saying before responding. It is natural for recruiters to become defensive when someone presents one or more objections. After all, the prospect is saying that he or she doesn't want to join the organization to which the recruiter is committed. However, getting into arguments is not the way to overcome objections.

When recruiting in a one-on-one situation you are presented with perhaps your best opportunity to show some empathy for the prospect. Listening is critical. The best advice for recruiters is in the famous passage "We were all given two ears and one mouth and we should use them in that proportion."

The All Time, Number One, Absolutely Best Way to Overcome Objections to Joining

Overcoming objections is always going to be a situational challenge. Each situation will be a little different and the following suggested responses are made for the specific objection being discussed.

There is **one** technique which can be used to overcome virtually any objection. This technique also re-emphasizes the importance of getting current members to help recruit new members. This technique is known as the *feel-felt-found* method and it's very simple. When prospects say that they think membership is too expensive or that they don't have time to participate, the person asking them to join simply says, "I know how you *feel*. I *felt* the same way myself, but I *found* that membership really was a great investment."

This method is obviously most effective when used by a member. In fact members are the only ones who can say that with any credibility. This method combines the real benefits of joining with the testimonial of someone who has already made the commitment. If there were no other reason for trying to get current members to help recruit, then the *feel-felt-found* method is reason enough. The ideal situation for overcoming objections is to have a prospective member giving objections to a member who at one time had the same objection but eventually joined. It's the most powerful form of empathy and your organization needs to use it as often as possible.

The Most Common Objections

The following objections are the most common ones heard in all organizations. However, every organization will face objections that are unique to it and its community, profession, or industry. These unique objections should also be anticipated so that when they come up the recruiter will be prepared for them. You should try to adapt the techniques described in this chapter to those situations and objections that are unique to your organization.

The suggested responses to these specific objections are given in the context of a one-on-one conversation about joining an organization that is similar to what volunteers or staff members might face during a membership campaign. The setting could be in a person's office, at a restaurant, in a booth at a trade show, or at one of your organization's meetings.

To make it easier to use the information on overcoming objections, this chapter has been structured in a format that shows each objection, followed by some things to consider that look beyond the basic objection and into some of the rationale behind the objection. There are then some comments about things to avoid when responding to these objections, as well as suggested responses to overcome each objection.

Objection: "That's a lot of money."

Things to consider: The most commonly heard objection is about the money. You need to be prepared to overcome it. When prospects say that it sure costs a lot to join, they haven't said that the organization isn't worth the money. They just said that the amount to join is quite high in their opinion. Don't consider this comment as a final decision not to join.

Things to avoid: The first thing many recruiters do is disagree. They try to convince the prospect that the cost of joining isn't a lot of money when you look at all of the things your organization does. This gives the prospect the feeling that you have just said that the prospect is wrong about whether or not it costs a lot to join. Even worse than telling the prospect he or she is wrong is the fact that the prospect gets the immediate feeling that you are *not listening!*

If the prospect thinks you are not listening there is little chance that the prospect will be convinced to join.

Another method that is often used to overcome the money objection is to compare the cost of joining to something else to which the prospect can relate. This technique is most often used by volunteer recruiters who may know the prospect on a personal basis. Trying to compare membership to something else rarely does the trick. Stick to the real benefits of membership as they apply to the specific prospect.

Suggested responses: What you need to do in this situation is *agree* with the prospect. If the prospect says that it costs a lot of money to join an organization, you need to respond by agreeing that it is a big investment. You need to explain that the dues reflect the amount of money it takes for the organization to deliver the programs and services that can help the prospect's business or career. Then explain how they can get a good return on such an investment.

Remember that you don't want to argue with the prospect over the *cost* of joining. It's not the amount of money to which people really object. It's the fact that they don't understand what value they are getting for their money. You want to be sure not to get bogged down in a discussion of the value of five hundred dollars or ten dollars or twenty dollars. First of all, it's an argument that you can't win. Value is a subjective thing and only the prospect can determine his or her perception of five hundred dollars or ten dollars worth of membership value. Secondly, why argue over the amount of money it costs to join when it can't be changed?

Money is almost always an issue so the best thing to do is acknowledge it. At the very least the prospect will know that you are listening. Agree with the prospect that it is a big investment, but suggest that it's the kind of investment that will be returned many times over.

Objection: "I don't have the time to participate."

Things to consider: Perhaps the second most frequently heard objection is that people don't have time. Prospects will say that they'd like to join your organization but they are just too busy to participate. They think that if they can't participate there's no sense in joining.

Things to avoid: When many recruiters hear this objection the tendency is to go right back into all of the basic reasons to join. They immediately start to tell the prospect about all the things that they'll gain if they just try to go to *one* meeting or participate in one program.

Don't tell the prospect how participating in programs and coming to meetings will benefit him or her because you were just told that the programs that require a physical presence are not of value to the prospect. This just reinforces to the prospect that you are not listening.

Suggested responses: Since lack of time is a common objection, you need to be prepared by having at least two lists of reasons to join in your mind when approaching potential members. One list should include those benefits members get from participating in organizational activities. This would include conventions, educational programs, seminars, workshops, and so on.

The other list consists of benefits members get even if they never leave their home or office. This would include things like publications, insurance programs, government relations programs, and video programs. This list is the one to focus on first when prospects say they are too busy. Let the prospect know that you understand how busy he or she is, and that fortunately there are reasons to join that don't include spending a lot of time attending meetings. These programs and services alone are worth the cost of membership.

This doesn't mean that you should ignore the benefits that require an investment of the member's time. It just means that you need to customize the way these benefits are described to this particular prospect.

Objection: "I don't like some of the organization's policies."

Things to consider: The fact that people don't like some of the policies of your organization is certainly understandable but it's not necessarily a reason for people not to join. They may not be familiar with the way policies are established in your organization.

Things to avoid: Don't be defensive about your organization's policies or positions. You aren't going to change them just to get this one prospect or group of prospects to join. When you try to defend specific positions of your organization, you risk getting away from the reason you are talking to the prospect in the first place, which is getting them to see the value of membership. Don't let the policy disagreement be the only benefit that you discuss.

Suggested responses: When somebody says that they have an objection to a position that your organization took on a particular issue, you need to tell him or her that you understand that there are two sides to just about every issue. One of the things you like to do in your organization is recruit people with different viewpoints so that you can hear both sides of the issue. The great thing about your organization is that it is a one-person, one-vote organization. In order to change policy the prospect needs to join and have his or her voice heard.

You also need to point out that there are opportunities to shape the organization's policies but those opportunities are reserved for dues-paying members. If the prospect really wants the organization to adopt his or her opinion, then joining is the best and only way to make that happen.

Objection: "I'm already a member of another organization."

Things to consider: Many individuals or companies are members of more than one organization, so it should be not surprise you when prospects say that they or their company are already members of too many organizations, or that they are already active in another organization. They may even indicate that one of these other organizations is one of your competitors.

Things to avoid: This situation can become a real trap for the recruiter. If the prospects say that they like your organization but they are already members of a competing organization, you need to be careful not to get caught in the position of comparing one organization to another organization. Without knowing it you may be talking to somebody who is very active or maybe even a current or past officer in that other organization. You need to be careful about saying anything negative about any competing organization. Even when you begin your response by complimenting the other group, don't make the mistake of saying in the next statement that it is a good group but it can't do for the prospect as much as your group can. This implies the other group is inferior and that the prospect made a mistake by joining.

Before making comparisons to other organizations you need to spend some time understanding who your competition is and what these organizations do. That way at least your facts will be correct when comparing benefits.

Suggested responses: When prospects say that they are already members of several other organizations, one of the things that you want to point out is the fact that many members of your organization are also members of more than one organization. This is because they believe that they get *different* benefits from each organization. If you know your competing organizations well enough, you can point out the *differences* between the organizations. You should avoid talking about programs where the two organizations overlap. After all, why would the prospect want to pay dues to two organizations to get the same benefits from both?

By pointing out the benefits your organization offers that competing groups don't, you can let the prospect draw the comparisons. Let the prospect know that joining more than one organization is something that is done all the time and that this new membership is an additional investment needed to get additional benefits. You are not asking the prospect to drop the membership in another organization to join yours.

Objection: "I've listened to what you're saying but I just don't see the benefit to me or my company."

Things to consider: When prospects say that they've heard what you're saying but just don't see the benefit, they are basically saying that you haven't said anything that they feel meets their needs. You haven't found out what it is about a prospect's company or an individual's career that can be helped by joining your organization.

It probably means you've described your organization's features and activities and haven't focused on its benefits.

Things to avoid: In this situation there is a temptation to ask the prospect what he or she would like the organization to do for him or her. This is a very difficult way to get people to join. When you ask the prospect to identify his or her key need it can appear as though you are going to say whatever it will take to get them to join. In general, people are very leery of this kind of approach.

Suggested responses: Rather than giving the prospects the impression that if they'll tell you what they'd like to hear you'll be glad to say it, a more effective response is needed. You could ask the prospect to put aside what you've already discussed, and try to envision starting a completely new organization. Ask the prospect to identify the very first thing this "new" organization could do to provide value to the prospect or the prospect's company. As the prospect describes what he or she would like to see happen in a "new" organization, the prospect is really describing exactly what he or she wants your organization to do for him or her. What they've done is to identify the benefits that they are seeking from *any* organization. This allows you to adapt your presentation so it highlights those specific programs or benefits that can best meet the prospect's primary needs.

Objection: "I get the benefits whether I join or not."

Things to consider: This objection is probably the most frustrating one you are going to hear. It is most frequently mentioned when discussing the benefits provided by legislative and advocacy programs that benefit the entire profession, industry, or community. What makes this objection especially frustrating is that fact that the prospect is correct that he or she WILL get the benefits whether he or she joins or not.

Things to avoid: When potential members say there is no need to join because they are going to get the benefits anyway, you need to avoid getting frustrated and upset. Try not to respond to the objection by telling prospects that you merely want them to contribute their fair share for the benefits your organization provides. This may seem like a rational response to the objection. It can seem particularly reasonable for a volunteer recruiter who may feel cheated because he or she is paying dues to provide benefits to the prospect who is not paying the dues, but it is actually a rather negative way to get people to join. When you make a statement like that, it almost sounds as if you are trying to get the prospect to join the organization out of a sense of guilt.

Suggested responses: By putting a slight twist on this response, you can put it on a more positive basis. When prospects say that they are going to get the benefit of the organization's efforts anyway, you need to think before you react. You might want to respond to prospects by saying they are right, or by agreeing that they or their company does get the benefit of what the organization is doing and that you are proud of the accomplishments of your organization. Tell the prospect it's not a question of being effective, it's a question of how much more effective the organization would be if it could represent the entire industry or profession or community rather than just the portion you currently represent through your existing members. Suggest that the prospect join for a year and see how much better off everyone will be when the whole industry or profession or community is united.

You need to reinforce to prospects that the benefits they are already experiencing would be even better if they and other nonmembers would join. It is a much more positive way to overcome the objection.

Objection: "We're cutting back." or "My employer won't pay."

Things to consider: These are certainly legitimate objections and you will hear them even more frequently in harsh economic times. This is another money-related objection and requires some empathy on the part of the recruiter. Remember that the prospect here hasn't said that he or she doesn't see any value in joining or that he or she doesn't like your organization. The prospect isn't even saying that it is too much money. He or she is just saying that it is difficult to find the money right now.

Things to avoid: Don't assume that this objection is the end of the conversation. Try not to become argumentative and don't keep going back to the basic list of activities and programs. Try to focus on the prospect's problem, which is finding the money to join.

Suggested responses: In the case of chambers and trade associations, you need to point out the fact that when times are tough and there doesn't seem to be much work available, information on what work is available can be found by joining your organization and meeting with your members. This reinforces the benefit of networking at your meetings and conventions. You can also talk about the fact that even though times may be tough right now they won't always be this way. If prospects join the organization now they can be in a position to take advantage of what will (hopefully) be a better economy in the future.

Another aspect of this objection you need to consider is that when prospects say that their companies are cutting back, they usually mean that they are cutting back on things such as memberships and contributions. You need to focus the discussion away from having them see membership as a contribution or charity. Tell the prospect that you understand that while budgets are being cut in some areas, one area that is probably not being affected is employee training. Get the prospect to think of membership in your organization as a valuable addition to his or her company's education and training program. Perhaps there is money in the training budget. You might also explain that membership in your organization is really a great addition to the prospect's marketing efforts. There may be enough in the marketing budget for the prospect to become a member now.

What you are trying to do is show prospects that the value of membership exists in many forms, and the money for membership may be available elsewhere in their company's budget.

The objection that the employer won't pay is one that is often heard in professional societies. In this case you need to remind the prospect that this is a personal investment in his or her own career and that he or she takes the membership and the benefits of membership with them wherever he or she goes.

If it becomes clear that the prospect is just not going to join at this time and you don't want to become too aggressive in forcing a decision, there is a final option. This option involves getting the prospect to agree that **if** the money were available he or she would join now. After getting this agreement you can thank the prospect for his or her time, find out when the prospect might be in a better position to join, and offer to put him or her on a mailing list to receive your organization's publications on a temporary basis. This will give him or her a taste of what being a member is like and will give you an opportunity to follow up periodically. It's not advisable to send the prospect everything that regular members get. If the prospect perceives that he or she is getting all of the member benefits without paying there is little incentive to join and pay for them.

Objection: "Someone else in our company or institution is already a member."

Things to consider: This objection is frequently heard by professional societies and other individual membership organizations. In this scenario the prospect believes that he or she is getting all the benefits through another person who works for the same employer.

Things to avoid: Be careful not to give the impression that you are trying to make the prospect feel guilty about taking advantage of someone else's investment.

Suggested responses: There are a couple of ways to attempt to overcome this objection. One approach is to remind the prospect that membership in the organization is a personal membership that can be carried from employer to employer. If the person in the company or institution who is currently a member changed jobs, where would the prospect get the benefits? In addition, there is an important benefit the prospect can't get through a co-worker and that's the ability to help his or her own career by interacting and networking with other members of the organization. If the prospect wants to get and maintain that advantage, the extra fee he or she would pay to attend meetings and conferences as a nonmember will quickly add up to more than the membership fee. It would probably be less expensive to just join.

A second approach is one that is becoming more effective as technology increases the speed of information transfer. This approach reminds the prospects that counting on someone else to give them valuable information means that they will get the information later than members do. Since this is an environment in which old information is often perceived to be less valuable information, the prospect really is at a disadvantage if he or she relies on someone else to get information. He or she would get the information sooner and in its original format by being a member.

Objection: "I was a member once before and didn't like it."

Things to consider: If this objection comes up unexpectedly then you probably haven't done enough research on the prospect before approaching him or her. This can be a very embarrassing objection to face because you are already telling the prospect to some extent that you don't know the person you are trying to recruit. This shows little or no personalization.

Things to avoid: The initial reaction to such a statement would usually be to ask the prospect either why he or she left the organization or what it was that they didn't like about the organization. However, both of these questions are going to get a negative answer and will put you on the defensive right away.

Suggested responses: If you are learning for the first time that the prospect is a former member, perhaps the best way to meet this objection would be to ask what was the last year that he or she was a member. By doing that you get the prospect to focus on a time frame rather than on a negative thought. If the prospect says that he or she has been out of the organization for more than one to two years, you have the opportunity to take control of the conversation by saying that you'd like to bring them up to date on some new and valuable benefits that have been added since he or she was last in the organization. In this manner you can concentrate on the positive new benefits of being a member now.

Objection: "I'd like to think it over."

Things to consider: This is somewhat of a variation of the "I just don't see the benefit" objection. It doesn't mean that the recruiter hasn't done a good job. It just means that the prospect doesn't want to make a decision at this time.

Things to avoid: Don't force the issue. There is a danger of coming across as an aggressive salesperson if you insist that the prospect make a decision right now. On the other hand, don't give up at the first mention of this desire to think it over.

Suggested responses: There are three ways to overcome this objection without seeming too aggressive. First, you can tell the prospect that you understand and you will be happy to get back to him or her. Then, ask when would be a good time to follow-up. Ask him or her to be as specific as possible about the date and time. This allows the prospect to feel that he or she isn't being pressured and allows you to pin down the time when a decision will be reached. Then you can ask if the prospect has any questions or would like any additional information sent before the selected time. If the prospect responds with a specific request, you will have the chance to show what great follow-up service the prospect is going to get when he or she joins.

Second, you can invite the prospect to attend an upcoming function to get a sample of the networking and other benefits of joining. This keeps the organization and the prospect involved with each other while the prospect thinks it over.

Finally, you can try to get the prospect to make a decision more quickly if there is an incentive to join now. This incentive might be a gift or a reduced-fee offering to new members who join by a certain date or even the ability to be in the organization's soon-to-be-published directory.

Objection: "I need to talk it over with someone else."

Things to consider: This is a universal objection and it even has its own name. This objection is known as the "taking it to a higher authority" objection. This objection is heard frequently in chambers of commerce when you approach prospective members whose businesses are part of a chain or franchise. Hotels, motels, restaurants, and retail stores are examples of businesses that will give this objection.

Things to avoid: Don't get caught by surprise. Do your homework and find out before you approach the prospect what the policy is in their particular organization.

Suggested responses: If you know that the prospective member is part of a chain or a franchise company, contact the company's regional or national headquarters and find out exactly what their policy is on joining trade groups, chambers of commerce or professional organizations. Many times the policy is to leave the decision to the local company's management or to the local franchise owner. If this is the case, you can pre-empt the objection by simply stating that you know that the parent company allows the local management to make these decisions and suggest that joining the chamber or trade or professional group makes good sense for the local affiliated business.

If the policy truly is to have the decision to join made by someone else, ask to speak to that person.

Try to get the prospect to agree that he or she would like to join and that all he or she needs to do is to get the approval of the higher authority. At least there is agreement on the fact that the prospect wants to join and will, if approval is given. Remind the prospects of their desire to join in a follow-up letter or phone call.

Objection: "We don't need any more business."

Things to consider: This is another objection that is frequently heard in chambers or trade groups. It is also heard in professional societies recruiting businesses which want additional market exposure as associate members. Overcoming this objection requires two of the skills discussed earlier: listening and displaying empathy.

Things to avoid: Don't indicate that you find this hard to believe - even if you do. After all, can the prospect really mean that he or she doesn't need any more customers? He or she probably means that business is good right now and he or she is having difficulty seeing the benefits of joining if that means more customers.

Suggested responses: If you are listening carefully to the objection, it is easy to pick up the fact that the prospect doesn't believe that the organization can help his or her business sell more products or services. Your job is to point out to prospects that just because they don't see the opportunity to make more sales through membership doesn't mean that there isn't an opportunity to make more profit through membership. This is where you need to point out the ways the organization can help reduce costs through such programs as training, insurance, government relations, and regulatory compliance.

No one can anticipate every possible objection and no one can expect to get every prospect to join. Overcoming objections is a skill. It is a skill that can be developed by knowing the most common objections and practicing effective techniques to overcome them.

Lessons learned:

- *objections exist in the minds of prospects regardless of the recruiting method used*
- *effective listening is a key to overcoming objections*
- *the best way to overcome most objections is to have current members use the "feel-felt-found" technique*

CHAPTER SEVEN
DEVELOPING MEMBERSHIP LITERATURE

What to look for in this chapter:
- *how to project a positive image for your organization in your membership literature*
- *what to include in your membership recruitment materials*
- *ideas for formatting your materials to get the greatest response*

Once you understand and can clearly express the benefits of joining your organization, you can develop materials to help you communicate those benefits to your prospective members. These materials include your organization's benefits brochure, membership application and other supporting materials. This chapter covers how to project an organizational image that is reflective of your members, how to determine what style membership brochure you want to develop and what to include in a membership brochure. It also covers how to customize your materials to attract specific targeted prospect groups, what the best ways are to use graphics, photos and colors in your materials, and finally, what to include on the membership application.

Projecting an Image For Your Organization

You must keep in mind that your organization's basic membership brochure will convey the *image* of your organization. It's the first thing prospects see that represents who you are and what you do. You need to be careful about what you put in your brochure. Remember that your image can be good or bad. You need to consider and review everything well ahead of time if you're going to make this brochure one that will present your organization in the most positive and effective way. If your image is one of an organization that tries to cut corners, then it's going to be difficult to get people to join. On the other hand, if your brochure looks too slick and forceful, it can also alienate some prospects. Your first consideration needs to be what kind of image you want to present.

One way to decide what image to project is to think about your members and what they do for a living. You might want your brochure to be reflective of your industry, profession, or community. If your organization is a scientific society, you might want to project an image that is in keeping with the particular field of study with which your members are involved, or with the image of their companies or institutions. If you are a chamber of commerce, you should think about the part of the country you're in, the size of your community, and the top local issues. Trade associations would want to present an image that is in keeping with the industry or businesses they serve. If you're not certain what your members consider to be an appropriate image, *ask them!* Put together one or two draft versions of your brochure and let your members tell you if the image you are projecting is one with which they would like to be associated. After all, they <u>are</u> going to be associated with it.

Another related but slightly different consideration is what is sometimes referred to as the culture of your organization. For purposes of developing membership literature, culture is defined as a more inward way of expressing the nature of your group. Culture includes not only your message but how your message is conveyed.

A professional society of technically-oriented people can probably get away with a little more written copy on a page than a trade association whose members are in sales or promotional work. For example, the membership brochure for a society of engineers might look entirely different than one for a society of public relations professionals, yet neither one would necessarily be better or worse than the other.

Design Options for Your Membership Brochure

Every organization has some sort of standard membership information brochure that they send or deliver to prospective members. A brochure that works for one organization might be completely wrong for another organization. As was the case with the reasons why members join, there is no magic formula for a good membership brochure.

The choices for designing a membership brochure are endless.

There are full-sized (8-1/2"x11") brochures, oversized brochures, brochures designed to fit in a standard mailing envelope, brochures that are folders, one-page brochures, and brochures that are actually booklets with ten or more pages. Some brochures are all-inclusive, meaning they are designed to include everything the prospect needs in one piece. This all-inclusive brochure could include a marketing message, an application, and a return envelope. Other brochures are designed solely to inspire the prospect to want to join and are accompanied by the materials necessary to do so.

Determining What Information to Include in Your Brochure

The most difficult part of developing membership literature actually isn't deciding what to include. You probably want to include everything you can about your organization and the benefits of joining, but that could mean you end up with a very large and confusing brochure. The real dilemma in preparing membership literature is deciding what, if anything, to leave out.

One very effective technique that can help you determine what to include in your brochure and in other membership literature is called the *need-to-know/nice-to-know* technique. Try to evaluate all of the information about your organization on the basis of whether the prospect needs to know the information in order to make the decision to join or whether it is just information that would be nice to know. Need-to-know information would normally include such things as your benefits statements, the cost of joining, and membership requirements. Nice-to-know information would include things like your organization's history and its current leadership. Once you have evaluated your information on this need-to know/nice-to-know basis, it will be easier to judge what really should go in your brochure and what information can be left out if necessary.

Describing Membership Benefits and Services

The most important element in the brochure is the presentation of membership benefits. These benefits statements need to demonstrate empathy for the person reading the brochure. Many organizations use some type of highlighting to make key benefits stand out. Among highlighting options are larger print, bold lettering, underlining, and bullets or arrows that point out important words or phrases.

Describing member services in a brochure is only effective when used as supporting statements for the benefits they help provide. For example, in a professional society you can highlight educational opportunities as a benefit of joining and then support that benefit statement by listing the various services or programs that provide education to members. This would include things such as your publications, educational conferences, and conventions or meetings.

If you wanted to highlight business development opportunities in a chamber of commerce brochure, you could support that benefit by listing the ways you help members promote their products and services. This would include listing such activities as after-hours mixers, advertising, and visitors' guides.

In a trade association, you might want to highlight the cost-saving benefits of membership. You can support that benefit statement by listing such programs as member discounts, reduced insurance fees, and legislative action.

When you list the programs and services that support your benefit statements, you not only give more credibility to the benefit, you also show the prospect that each of your programs and services has a real purpose. That's an important way to show that you're not going to waste their dues investment on programs that don't benefit them.

Using Testimonials in Your Membership Brochure

A testimonial is a statement made by a member of your organization that says something positive about your organization. Ideally, in this statement the member will go beyond the fact that he or she thinks you are a good organization and will actually say that membership in the organization has been beneficial to him or her in a specific way.

Using testimonials to sell products and services has been a standard practice in the private sector since the beginning of the use of modern marketing techniques. There is no reason why not-for-profit organizations should not do the same. People listen to other people they respect, admire, or envy. That's why celebrities are paid large sums of money to endorse products. Not-for-profit organizations have a built-in opportunity to get testimonials about the value of membership by using their current members.

You should try to use at least one quote from an active member in your membership brochure. This can be in the form of a general statement, or a statement supporting a specific benefit. The specific message you're trying to communicate will determine which member or members to quote. In some cases, quoting a leader in your trade, community, or profession is a good way to add credibility to your overall message. In other cases you'd want to quote someone or some company who has benefited from a specific service. Some organizations add a testimonial statement to each benefit section of their brochure.

If you use testimonials, there are two things you want to try to accomplish. One is to get the testimonial from people or companies who have credibility with the readers, either because they are well-known and respected or because they can testify to the value of a specific program or service. The other thing you'd like to accomplish, if possible, is to have testimonials that *quantify* the benefit received from the service. These testimonial comments could talk about the amount of money a company saved by getting the member discount when attending an educational program. That would have more impact than just the fact that the educational programs existed.

As with the other information in printed materials, testimonials can get outdated. That means that if you've quoted a specific individual or company there is a chance that the testimonial will lose it's credibility over time if the person quoted retires from the company or field, changes affiliations, or gets fired. At that point you've lost much of the value of the quote. To avoid the possibility of outdated materials you can either develop a brochure with easy-to-update inserts or you can include your testimonials in your cover letter.

Explaining How to Join

Somewhere in the brochure you need to get the point across that you want the prospect to *join* your organization. Some organizations believe, because of the image they want to project, they need to avoid taking an aggressive sales approach in their brochure. This is certainly understandable, but it avoids the central question of what you want the prospect to *do* with the information that the brochure provides. As in the sale of anything, if you don't ask the prospects to take action there is little chance they will.

You should use language that shows you really want the member to join. Specifically, you need to make it easy for the reader to understand *how* to join. Some organizations have strict requirements for membership, such as education, designation, length of time in the field, or geographic location. These criteria need to be listed. If your organization has a formal membership approval process, you should mention this in your literature, too.

The format of the actual membership application also needs to be considered. If it is a separate piece it must be referred to in the brochure. If it is part of the brochure, it needs to be formatted in a way that allows it to be detached easily.

For some organizations the application is, by necessity, a rather long and complicated form. This is usually the case when there are highly specific requirements for membership that need to be documented or when the applicant needs to provide a list of references. Sometimes the application is long and involved simply out of tradition.

In some cases the application can actually be a barrier to membership because of its complexity. By nature, most people are unwilling to give out any more information about themselves or their company than is necessary. In order to increase your response rate on membership solicitations, it is recommended that you keep the application as simple as possible. Simplification of the application is another example of the need-to-know/nice-to-know theory. Get the information that is absolutely essential to approving the application at the time you ask a prospect to join, and make that process as simple and quick as possible. The other information can be gathered after they've become a member. In fact, this need to gather further information about demographics, business interests, experience, and other matters is a good excuse to make that all-important follow-up contact <u>after</u> the applicant joins.

Cost-effective Ways to Customize Membership Literature

Many of the considerations in deciding what style of brochure to use are based on resources. Organizations with larger budgets have more flexibility and can afford to take some chances with higher-cost features such as color and ungraded paper quality. These larger groups can also develop a different brochure for each of their various target markets. They can try different formats with different markets depending upon what is appropriate for that particular market. A target market is a smaller subset of your entire prospect base that has been identified according to one or more specific factors, such as company size, professional specialty, or geographic location.

Having limited resources doesn't mean that your organization can't produce an effective brochure. It just means that your organization has to be more careful in making its decision on what to produce. Smaller organizations will also find that they don't have the luxury of producing a different brochure for each target market. This may mean that the organization needs to cover the membership benefits of several markets or even all markets in one piece.

One inexpensive way to customize membership literature is by using what is called a *step brochure.* This is a brochure that has information inside a folder with pockets on either side. Normally the pocket on one side contains samples of your organization's literature, such as newsletters, magazines, and other materials. The other pocket contains a series of one-page inserts with information about the organization, such as its history, structure, and membership procedures. These inserts are arranged in a step-like fashion with each succeeding insert cut to enable the reader to see the heading on each additional piece. These headings could include such things as "Membership Benefits", "How to Join", "A Guide to Services", and so on.

There are two benefits of this type of brochure, particularly for smaller organizations. The brochure can be customized for each target market by simply changing the inserts. You can have different inserts that describe the benefits in a way that is geared toward each of your target markets and use whichever one is applicable to that particular group. The other benefit of the step brochure is that it is relatively inexpensive to update. As your information changes you can simply print new inserts instead of throwing out all of the out-dated brochures and starting over again

Another option for customizing your membership literature is through a cover letter. Sending an effective cover letter with your membership literature allows you to guide prospects to the benefits in the brochure that apply directly to them or their company.

Using Graphics, Photos, and Color in Your Membership Literature

It's a fact that most people scan brochures and other written materials before deciding if they want to read them in detail. If your brochure consists solely of page after page of uninterrupted copy, you aren't really showing any awareness of how most people receive and absorb written information. The main reason that there is too much copy in most brochures is that organizations generally try to put too much nice-to-know information in their literature. Remember that the brochure needs to be assessed based on the whole package of considerations and not just on how much information can be crammed into one piece.

Using graphics, photos, or color in your brochure has several advantages for your organization. These advantages include the fact that these options break up the copy and help the flow of the material. They can also help the prospect envision some of the benefits and raise the image of your material and your organization to a higher level of quality. In addition, they can draw attention to key benefit statements.

It's not necessary to have color photos or graphics in your materials to add credibility to your message. Your organization's image will dictate what is appropriate. Cost is one of the biggest considerations when deciding whether or not to use certain graphics or color. The addition of any new color adds to the cost of repro-duction and needs to be considered when budgeting for the material. Your organization needs to determine or estimate how much of the decision to join is based on the membership materials prospects receive. The more important your membership material is to your recruitment efforts, the more important the decision will be on where and when to add color, photos, or graphics to your brochures.

Lessons learned
- *your membership literature is the first impression prospects get of your organization, so consider it carefully*
- *use the need-to-know/nice-to-know concept to determine what to include in your literature*
- *raise the effectiveness of your materials by customizing and adding graphics or color*

SAMPLE 7-A
This is a membership brochure produced by a chamber of commerce.

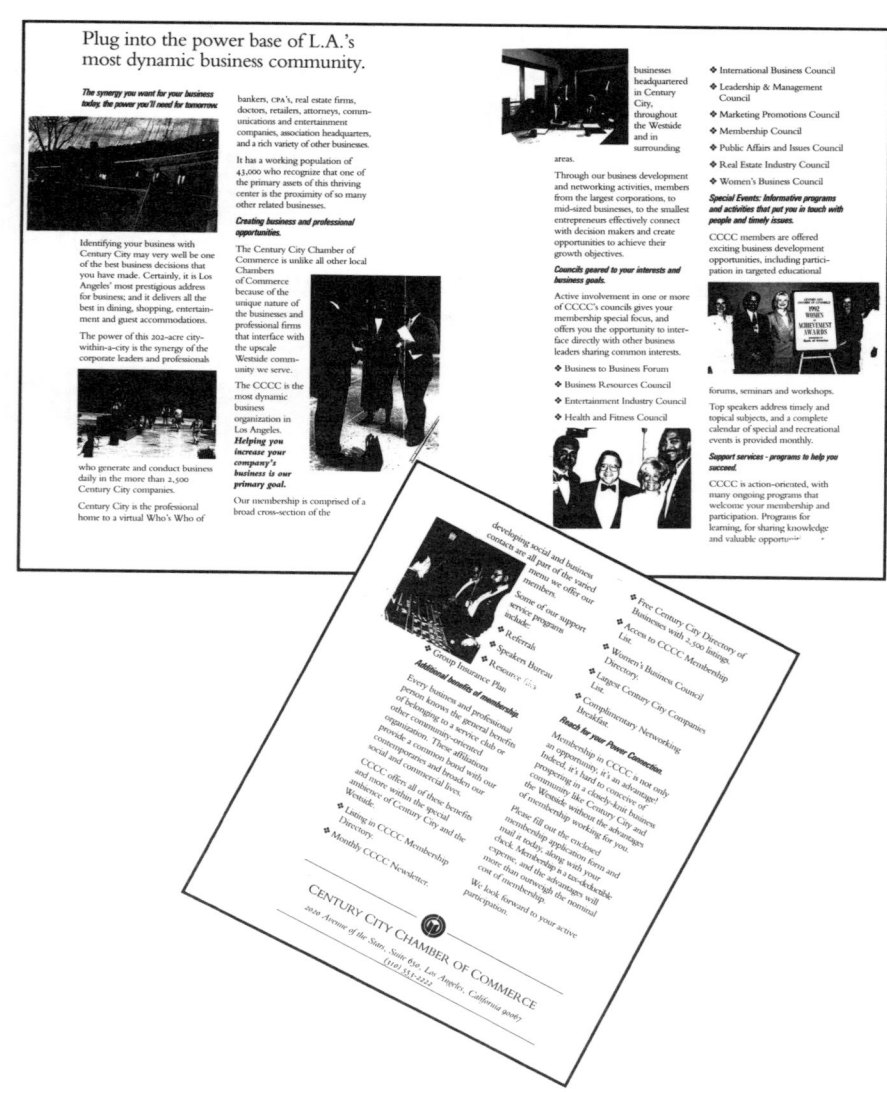

Plug into the power base of L.A.'s most dynamic business community.

The synergy you want for your business today, the power you'll need for tomorrow.

Identifying your business with Century City may very well be one of the best business decisions that you have made. Certainly, it is Los Angeles' most prestigious address for business; and it delivers all the best in dining, shopping, entertainment and guest accommodations.

The power of this 202-acre city-within-a-city is the synergy of the corporate leaders and professionals who generate and conduct business daily in the more than 2,500 Century City companies.

Century City is the professional home to a virtual Who's Who of bankers, CPA's, real estate firms, doctors, retailers, attorneys, communications and entertainment companies, association headquarters, and a rich variety of other businesses.

It has a working population of 43,000 who recognize that one of the primary assets of this thriving center is the proximity of so many other related businesses.

Creating business and professional opportunities.

The Century City Chamber of Commerce is unlike all other local Chambers of Commerce because of the unique nature of the businesses and professional firms that interface with the upscale Westside community we serve.

The CCCC is the most dynamic business organization in Los Angeles. *Helping you increase your company's business is our primary goal.*

Our membership is comprised of a broad cross-section of the businesses headquartered in Century City, throughout the Westside and in surrounding areas.

Through our business development and networking activities, members from the largest corporations, to mid-sized businesses, to the smallest entrepreneurs effectively connect with decision makers and create opportunities to achieve their growth objectives.

Councils geared to your interests and business goals.

Active involvement in one or more of CCCC's councils gives your membership special focus, and offers you the opportunity to interface directly with other business leaders sharing common interests.

❖ Business to Business Forum
❖ Business Resources Council
❖ Entertainment Industry Council
❖ Health and Fitness Council

❖ International Business Council
❖ Leadership & Management Council
❖ Marketing Promotions Council
❖ Membership Council
❖ Public Affairs and Issues Council
❖ Real Estate Industry Council
❖ Women's Business Council

Special Events: Informative programs and activities that put you in touch with people and timely issues.

CCCC members are offered exciting business development opportunities, including participation in targeted educational forums, seminars and workshops. Top speakers address timely and topical subjects, and a complete calendar of special and recreational events is provided monthly.

Support services - programs to help you succeed.

CCCC is action-oriented, with many ongoing programs that welcome your membership and participation. Programs for learning, for sharing knowledge and valuable opportunities

developing social and business contacts are all part of the varied menu we offer our members.

Some of our support service programs include:

❖ Referrals
❖ Speakers Bureau
❖ Resource List

Additional benefits of membership

Group Insurance Plan

Every business and professional person knows the general benefits of belonging to a service club or other community-oriented organization. These affiliations provide a common bond with our contemporaries and broaden our social and commercial lives.

CCCC offers all of these benefits and more within the special ambience of Century City and the Westside.

❖ Listing in CCCC Membership Directory.
❖ Monthly CCCC Newsletter.

❖ Free Century City Directory of Businesses with 2,500 listings
❖ Access to CCCC Membership List
❖ Women's Business Council
❖ Largest Century City Companies Directory.
❖ Complimentary Networking Breakfast

Reach for your Power Connection.

Membership in CCCC is not only an opportunity, it's an advantage! Indeed, it's hard to conceive of prospering in a closely-knit community like the Century City and the Westside without the advantages of membership working for you.

Please fill out the enclosed membership application form and mail it today, along with your check. Membership is a tax-deductible expense. The advantages will more than outweigh the nominal cost of membership.

We look forward to your active participation.

CENTURY CITY CHAMBER OF COMMERCE
2020 Avenue of the Stars, Suite 850, Los Angeles, California 90067
(310) 553-2222

SAMPLE 7-B
This is a membership brochure of an international professional society.

Discover your professional association

Now that you've chosen physical therapy as your career, put the profession's association to work for you! Join the American Physical Therapy Association (APTA), the national organization dedicated to serving the physical therapy profession. It's the ideal way to learn about your chosen career and the many practice options open to you.

Keep up with new developments

APTA is your best source for the latest information on physical therapy practice, trends, and issues. Four information-packed publications, including

- *PT—Magazine of Physical Therapy,*
- *Physical Therapy,*
- *PT Bulletin,*

and, especially for students,

- *Today's Student in PT,*

keep you abreast of professional developments. Changes and advances are occurring daily that aren't even in your textbooks...let APTA fill in the gaps!

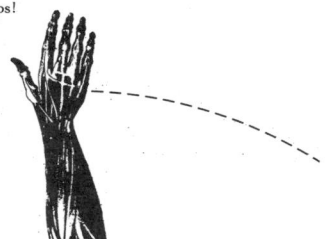

Get answers when you need them

Working on an important paper? Researching a complex new technique? Looking for sources of financial assistance for school? Help is just one phone call away! APTA can get you the answers you need. FREE bibliographies on topics like carpal tunnel syndrome, computer software and designing a physical therapy department are instantly available. And when you need more specialized details, a Medline computer search can be done for you—at a special member price of just $10!

Make professional contacts

You'll make new friends and lifelong contacts when you join APTA. You'll have a chance to share your ideas with other students at chapter and district meetings...at APTA's national conferences...at the dynamic National Student Conclave—the *only* national meeting for students of physical therapy. Your membership puts you in touch with the profession's leaders—policymakers, academicians, researchers, clinicians—who share your interests and concerns.

SAMPLE 7-C
This is a sample of a membership brochure developed by a trade association.

nasfm
NATIONAL ASSOCIATION OF STORE FIXTURE MANUFACTURERS

**NASFM Membership:
a business investment which
improves your bottom line!**

It's time to
take a close
look at all of
the benefits!

Market your company and products at The Store Fixturing Show

Each spring NASFM sponsors The Store Fixturing Show, a three-day event which consists of exhibits of more than 300 fixture companies as well as educational sessions. The visitors include about 7,000 retail fixture buyers and specifiers; store planners and designers; interior architects; and consumer product manufacturers. The Store Fixturing Show is produced by NASFM Associate Member "Display & Design Ideas" magazine.

Bottom-Line Benefit: As a member in good standing of NASFM, your company saves $4 to $5 per sq. ft. on exhibit space. This savings can easily offset the annual membership dues. More importantly, exhibiting at The Store Fixturing Show exposes your company and products to important fixture buyers and others who influence fixture purchases.

Education at seminars & plant tours

The Association sponsors various types of educational seminars to expose members to the latest information, techniques, and methods. Seminar topics include manufacturing, financial management, automation, costing and estimating, environmental compliance, and marketing. To provide members with the opportunity to observe production techniques, study the use of new or improved equipment, and exchange ideas on efficient plant operation, tours of members' plants are scheduled as part of the annual manufacturing seminar. In addition, NASFM conducts a reception and meeting in conjunction with the biannual International Woodworking Machinery & Furniture Supply Fair (IWF).

Bottom-Line Benefit: You and your employees stay on the leading edge of your profession, and gain a competitive advantage by learning the latest techniques at NASFM seminars.

Networking gives you an edge

At conventions, meetings, seminars, and other events the Association provides forums for bringing members together in an atmosphere conducive to good fellowship. In this atmosphere, members share their challenges and solutions with one another.

Bottom-Line Benefit: By attending these events, you develop personal and business relationships which improve individual and company performance.

Membership Directory promotes your company

The directory of NASFM members—which is especially designed for retailers and fixture buyers and specifiers, store planners and designers, and interior architects—is published annually and distributed to members and the fixture marketplace. Many fixture buyers compile their supplier lists from the companies listed in the NASFM directory. Associate Members may place advertising in the directory.

Bottom-Line Benefit: You are recognized as one of the nation's leading fixture manufacturers. This exposure could help generate sales inquiries. NASFM distributes thousands of copies of the directory to fixture buyers, who will see your company listing. In addition, NASFM members use the directory to identify potential subcontractors.

Other directories provide sales leads

Each year the Association also publishes the "Directory of Store Planners, Interior Designers, and Architects," which lists more than 1,200 design firms in North America. Periodically, NASFM also publishes directories of store fixture buyers. These directories are distributed to all NASFM member firms.

Bottom-Line Benefit: The directories can be used by your marketing and sales staff to contact potential fixture buyers.

"The NASFM News" keeps you informed

"The NASFM News" is the official bimonthly publication of the Association and contains current news items relative to meetings, services, and activities of NASFM. It also features information about equipment and plants for sale, help-wanted ads, and general news of interest to store fixture manufacturers.

Bottom-Line Benefit: By reading "The NASFM News" you will stay abreast of the latest information in your industry association, information which will help you define your markets and strategies.

Chapter Eight-
EFFECTIVE COVER LETTERS

What to look for in this chapter:
- *how people read their mail*
- *the most important parts of an effective cover letter*
- *how to use your cover letter to customize and personalize*
- *ideas to get more people to read your cover letter*

Whether on its own or as part of a package of information, a good cover letter can determine how successful your membership mailings will be. A cover letter is the term used for any letter included in your membership mailings that attempts to highlight specific benefits mentioned in other literature or to personalize and customize a membership mailing. In this chapter suggestions will be made on how to develop a cover letter that will get your organization's message across to the prospect in the most effective way.

Research by direct mail specialists indicates that most people read their mail in a very specific order. They first look at to whom the letter is sent. This is called the greeting or salutation. The next thing people do is look to see who the letter is from by looking at who signed the letter. Then people read the postscript, or P.S., if there is one. They read the P.S. because their eyes are already at the end of the letter. After that they go back and read the main portion, or body, of the letter if they still have interest.

This chapter covers the development of a cover letter in that order. It discusses other techniques for getting the interest of the prospect. These techniques include having a good opening statement or question, using statistics, having testimonials or quotes, methods for highlighting key points in the letter, using incentives to recruit members, and having an effective closing statement.

The salutation is important since it is the first impression the prospect will get and makes the way you begin your letter critical to its acceptance. Wherever possible you should address your letter to a person rather than to a company or some general category into which the prospect falls. People like to be treated as individuals, not as categories. Remember that the cover letter sends signals to prospects about how they are going to be treated after they join. If their first impression is that the organization is impersonal then it will be extremely difficult to convince them to join.

Another consideration in the salutation is formality. You have to determine if you should address the prospect by first name or last name. There are at least two factors that can help you decide about formality. One is the accepted practice in your organization and the industry, profession, or community you serve. If most of the people in your organization are addressed in day-to-day situations by title, then that's how your letter should address them. Be very careful if this is the case. People work hard to earn their designations so you need to be sure you're working with the most recent and most accurate information. If accepted practice in your organization is to address people by their first names then that's how you begin the letter.

Another way to determine how formal the salutation should be is to look at who will sign the letter and what their relationship is to the prospect. If the letter is going to a long list of prospects who are being contacted the first time and will be signed by the staff director or membership director, then it probably means the salutation should be more formal. If the letter is being signed by an elected leader who is well-known in the industry, community, or profession then it might be reasonable to use first names. You need to use both the accepted practice and the credibility of the signer in determining what type of salutation to use. In international organizations you will need to think about the accepted practices of the different countries you want to contact. In most non-U.S. countries the business salutation is formal.

One final note about the salutation. When you attempt to personalize the cover letter there is a risk of getting something wrong. It could be the person's name, title, or address. When you start off your letter with an error, you've severely hurt your chances of getting a favorable reply. Some organizations with large numbers of prospective members prefer to do less personal letters because of the time and expense involved with personalizing letters only to get many wrong. In most cases the additional cost and risk of personalizing the cover letter will be offset by a higher response rate than letters that do not mention a person's name in the salutation.

The signature can help establish the credibility of the cover letter. In some organizations the staff director may be more well known than the current volunteer leaders. In this case the staff director's signature will have some impact on the prospect's perception of the organization.

Having a volunteer leader sign the letter adds credibility because the signing member has already joined. They are just asking the prospect to do what as an industry, community, or professional peer they have already done. The signing member can also assist in the personalization and customizing if he or she is from the same specialty area or geographic area as the prospect . The very fact that a member is willing to sign a recruitment letter is a testimonial to the organization since it indicates that the signer is proud to have his or her name associated with the organization. If there is some doubt about who has the most credibility with the prospect, there is nothing wrong with having dual signatures such as both the staff director and an appropriate member.

The postscript, or P.S., is almost always read, so having one is advisable because it will be in the normal flow for the reader. It should also convince the prospect to reconsider the letter's overall message. An effective use of the postscript is to repeat the offering of any incentive that you have listed in the body of the letter. This will get the prospect to go back and start reading the letter from the opening to determine exactly what this incentive entails and who can qualify for it.

After reading the salutation, the signature, and the closing, the prospect will go back to read the rest of the letter. The **opening statement** in your cover letter needs to get the message across to the readers that you know who they are and what they do and that your organization can help them. In other words, you've got a very short period of time after the prospects begin reading the letter to convince them of your *empathy*. When your letter begins by listing the history and features of your organization you risk losing the readers' attention right away. If your benefit statements are buried in the middle of your letter they may never even be seen by a prospect who has already thrown the letter away. You need to consider doing something a little different to get the prospect's attention. Three techniques that have been used effectively are opening the letter with a question, using statistics, and beginning the letter with a quote.

Starting your cover letter with a question lets you get the reader involved in the letter right away. You should ask questions that relate to the prospect, not to the organization. These questions should also be worded so that the reader's responses to them will be positive.

In a trade association you might ask questions like "Wouldn't it be great if there was an organization that really understood the challenges a small business faces when trying to make a profit in this economy?"

In a chamber of commerce the questions might include such things as "Wouldn't it be nice if someone could help keep the city council from taxing small retailers out of business?"

In professional societies this opening question might be "Wouldn't it be nice if there was an organization to protect our right to practice the way we see fit?"

The answer to all of these questions is going to be affirmative. By getting the prospect to think this way, you start your letter by getting them to give you positive feedback. The prospect also wants to keep reading to see who or what it is that can do these things. By asking these types of specific questions you are telling the prospect that you must really know what it's like to be in his or her position. After asking two or three targeted questions, you can move into the body of your letter by telling the prospect that there is one organization that can do all these things and more. That organization is your organization!

Sometimes a statistic that relates to what the prospect does for a living can grab his or her attention at the beginning of a letter. Rather than starting off your letter by saying that your organization works every day to protect business at the local, state, and federal levels, you could start your benefits message by saying "Two thousand dollars! That may not sound like much to a bureaucrat in Washington but it sure means a lot to a small businessperson here in our community. That's how much money every member of our organization saved, on average, through our programs last year." The statistics here help show empathy, impact, and effectiveness.

Quoting an authoritative or recognizable source at the beginning of your letter is a way to add credibility to it right away. It also gets the reader wondering about the connection between the quote and the rest of the letter. You might start off with something like, "When Benjamin Franklin said 'A penny saved is a penny earned,' he might have been referring to our organization because we helped save our members a *lot* of their hard-earned pennies last year. We'd like to do the same for your company, too."

The body of the letter needn't repeat every benefit in the brochure if your brochure is an effective one. If prospects have to read through several paragraphs before figuring out what you want them to *do* with the information then you've put too much in the cover letter. Get to the point! Be sure that somewhere in the body of the letter you ask the prospects to join! You don't want them to think about joining or to agree that your organization has a lot to offer. You want them to join now.

The body of your letter should start off by supporting your opening statement with some additional facts or even a testimonial. Then it should move into some additional benefit statements that apply to this particular person, company, or category. If you're personalizing your letters, try mentioning the person's name at least one other time in the body of the letter to remind the reader that you know exactly who he or she is.

Highlighting is a method you may want to try in your letter to emphasize some of the more important parts. This would include arrows, underlines, asterisks, or anything that lets you draw attention to key points.

Using testimonials is another important option to keep in mind when developing a cover letter. You can mention the name of a prominent member of your organization or you can mention the name of the person that asked you to write to this particular prospect and refer to specific benefits they received as a result of being a member. One of the best ways to get people to recognize the value of your organization is to let them hear from their peers why they ought to join. Some organizations have tried using the entire cover letter as a testimonial by having the letter come directly from a member on his or her letterhead. In addition to establishing credibility for the organization, it raises the chances that the prospect will open the letter since it is coming from a peer.

The use of **incentives** is one of the most frequently used methods to add impact to the body of the letter. An incentive is simply a special offer that is made to the prospect for joining the organization. It's important to add a time element to the incentive because if the prospect can obtain the incentive anytime then even though there may be an incentive to join, there is no real incentive to join *now*. Incentives can include reduced dues, free organizational gifts or materials such as coffee mugs or pens, additional member-only discounts on meetings and conventions, free publications, or educational offerings. Some groups offer a specific dollar incentive that new members can use if they join now. If incentives are carefully planned and implemented, they can play a big role in membership recruitment.

The closing is the last part of the letter and should be where you summarize what you've said earlier in a short, effective manner. You might want to try enumerating some key benefits again by mentioning a few key words. This might also be the place to insert your incentive message. Always end the letter by thanking the reader for her or his interest and stating how much you're looking forward to welcoming him or her as your organization's newest member.

Lessons learned

- *the cover letter is the best way to customize your membership materials*

- *try to write with the prospect's priorities in mind*

- *pay special attention to salutation, the signature, and the P.S.*

- *using incentives can help get prospects to make the decision to join*

SAMPLE 8-A
Sample cover letter sent to a prospective member in a professional society.

Dear Ms Prospect,

Wouldn't it be great if you could improve your professionalism overnight?

What if you could access ALL of the latest industry information to help you do a better job?

What if you could have sample contracts and standards guidelines for almost every situation for **FREE?**

Wouldn't it be wonderful if you could call on other professionals who can help you get through the tough times? You could - by using your Membership Directory - a **FREE** membership service!

The choice is yours. Join the ABC society today - the best bargain in the field. Send in the enclosed membership application with your dues payment. You should also mark your selections on the New Member **FREE** publications list. These will be sent to you in your ABC New Member packet.

We look forward to hearing from you soon.

Sincerely,

Peter Practitioner,
President

P.S. Don't forget your **FREE** new member publication choice!

SAMPLE 8-B
Cover letter used by a trade association in a mailing to prospective members.

Dear Mr. Prospect,

Thank you for your interest in our Association. The enclosed brochure describes the many benefits our members get, but this letter is about YOU, the CEO.

Not surprisingly, companies large and small are included in our membership. Large companies like Gigantic Industries and smaller firms like Tinytown, Inc. are among our most active members. They've discovered that our Association is a great place to do two things that can help their success – meet potential customers and get new ideas.

Firms of all sizes attend our programs and share their success stories. You can learn from these people, be with the top firms in the industry, and pick up additional business. If there are any new ideas, new products, or new ways to approach an old challenge, you can find out about them at our meetings.

You can also get useful information from our extensive publications library, one of our most popular benefits. The most useful part of the library may be our catalogue of Award Winning Projects, the very best the industry has to offer.

Membership dues are based on the size of your company, with four categories based on your number of employees. For a company of your size (150-500 employees) your first year's dues would be $1,500.00. *If you join before October 30, you'll receive two free months of membership.*

To become a member, all you need to do is fill out the enclosed membership application and return it along with your first year's dues. That way you can begin to take advantage of the cost-saving and income-producing member-only programs right away.

We look forward to welcoming Appleton Industries as our newest member. We hope we'll get to present your Membership Plaque at our upcoming Annual Meeting in San Juan. Meeting information is enclosed.

Sincerely,

Bill Williams,
President

P.S. Don't forget the two free months membership if you join NOW!

SAMPLE 8-C
This sample cover letter was sent to prospects by a Chamber of Commerce.

Dear Mr. Prospect,

Would you pay a **dollar a day** to have someone on your staff who could help you increase your sales? And what would you say if we told you that that same person could show you a dozen ways to reduce your operating costs? That "staff member" is ready to go to work for you RIGHT NOW. It's the Central City Chamber of Commerce, and we really mean it when we say we want to work for you.

You see, Mr. Prospect, the way we look at it, you really don't join the Chamber – you HIRE us. And we take our work very seriously.

The Chamber works to increase your sales through our Buyers' Guides, our After Hours Programs, and our advertising opportunities. We help you keep your costs under control through our mangement education programs, our government relations efforts, and our Member-to-Member discounts. When we do those two things - increase your sales and reduce your costs - we are helping you do one more thing - **make a profit** in a higly competitive marketplace.

An additional benefit of Chamber membership is the chance to show your real support for your community. Chamber members appreciate that support, and make every attempt to do business with fellow members.

The enclosed information gives you more details about these programs and other Chamber benefits. Please fill out the enclosed membership application and return it along with your first year's dues TODAY. Why wait any longer to hire the Chamber to help your company grow? In fact, if you do join today you'll be able to take advantage of our new member ad opportunity. You'll get a free business card ad in our next Chamber newsletter. That's a $475 return on your dues investment right off the bat. How's that for a new "employee" getting off to a good start?

We look forward to welcoming you as our newest Chamber member.

Sincerely,

Charlene Jones, President
P.S. Don't forget that free ad!

CHAPTER NINE
Using Direct Mail Programs to Recruit New Members

What to look for in this chapter:
- *how to differentiate between solicitation mailings and informational mailings*
- *how to develop direct mail packages that get opened, read, and answered*
- *ways to measure and control the quality of your mailings*

Every organization has some type of information or recruitment literature that can be sent to interested prospects. Direct mail is and will continue to be a useful way to get your benefits message across to prospects. In this chapter you will be introduced to a number of important aspects of direct mail membership recruiting that you need to keep in mind if your efforts are going to be successful. This chapter covers the purposes of various types of mailings, how to determine what and when to mail, segmenting and targeting your markets, the frequency of mailings, putting together the various elements of a good membership recruitment package, and techniques for assuring that your mailings get maximum response through quality control.

Having a Clear Purpose to Your Mailings

A direct mail program is a program that includes a series of mailings to prospective members with a specific outcome intended. This outcome could be either increasing the number of membership applications returned or raising prospects' awareness of and interest in the organization and its benefits. Increasing new member applications is called a solicitation mailing and raising prospects' awareness is called an informational mailing. Before deciding what to include in your mailings to prospective members you need to decide which of these mailings you are going to do.

Remember that with a **solicitation mailing** the purpose is getting prospects to actually join your organization because of what they received in the mail. In that case you should consider that you are asking the prospect to open your material, read the material, understand it, like it, make the decision to join, fill out the application, fill out a check or credit card information, put the information in an envelope, put a stamp on the envelope, address it, and mail it back to you. That's a lot to ask of somebody just because of something received in the mail. That doesn't mean that recruiting through the mail won't work. It does mean that in order to get a good response rate to these mailings you'll need to have a very effective package of material.

The second type of mailing is the **informational mailing** where the purpose is to get the message of the organization in front of the prospects and raising their level of interest. The idea is to make them more receptive when the organization follows up through other methods such as the telephone or personal visits. Both types of mailings are worth doing but sometimes organizations get confused about which mailing they've done. Some groups put out an excellent informational mailing and are disappointed when they don't get a lot of new member applications back. That's because they didn't send a good solicitation mailing.

Determining What, When and How Often To Mail

The questions most frequently asked about direct mail programs are how many mailings to make to a prospect or group of prospects before giving up, what to send in your mailings, and when to send the mailings. There are no answers to these questions that will apply to every situation.

Some organizations use what is called the "buy-or-die" method of direct mail recruiting. This means they are going to send everything they have to everyone who qualifies to join until they either join the organization or die. If you have unlimited resources buy-or-die can be an effective method of direct mail recruitment. If your organization doesn't have unlimited resources, you need to gather as much information as possible about what direct mail method might work for you before deciding how many mailings to do and how much money to spend on those mailings. The most effective way to gather this information is by testing your mailings.

Testing involves measuring the response rates of various aspects of your mailing package against other aspects. For example, one aspect of your direct mail program that you can test is the envelope in which you send your mailings. In order to determine what size envelope is likely to get the best response rate on a mailing to 5,000 prospects, you might first do a test mailing of two different sized envelopes to a small group of prospects. Keep track to see which of the two sizes produces the highest return rate. By doing this, you'll find out what works best for you before committing all of your resources to one size. Other aspects of your mailing package that can be tested to help you anticipate response rates are different cover letters, different signatures on the cover letter, the timing of the mailings, various return envelopes, and combinations of enclosures. Once you have established some accurate testing results, you can spend your organization's marketing resources more effectively.

Another factor to consider in determining what to send to your prospects is whether or not you are able to identify specific segments of your market. A *market segment* is a portion of your total prospective member group that is identified by one or more demographic characteristics. When mailing to specific market segments you can customize your mailings to highlight benefits that would be most attractive to that particular segment.

The more market segments you can identify the more you can use *target marketing* to focus your efforts. Target marketing refers to the technique of developing different membership marketing messages for each of your identified market segments. In some organizations there might be only one or two target markets, such as large companies and small companies in a trade association or chamber of commerce. In other organizations there could be several, such as new graduates, private practitioners, government employees, or institutional workers in a professional society.

Determining how many mailings to make and how often to mail is difficult. This is an aspect of direct mail that really does call for some effective test mailings. Before determining what you think is the appropriate number of mailings for your recruitment efforts, you should do several test mailings to small groups of prospects and track your responses carefully. See if the first, second, third, or fourth mailing gets the highest response. Also check to see at what point the responses start to drop off dramatically. This will help you determine how many mailings to send to your full prospect list. If you do a series of four mailings and after the third mailing your response rate is not even covering the cost of the mailings, then you might want to limit your full prospect mailing to a series of three.

Regardless of how many mailings you decide to do, repeat mailings are a must. Very few people join after just one approach through the mail, so you'll need to plan ahead and budget for more than one mailing to each of your prospects or groups of prospects. You also need to think about what you're going to include in each mailing. There is no law that says each mailing in a series has to be exactly like the previous one in style, content, or timing.

Getting the Prospect to Open the Mailing

It's going to be pretty difficult to get a high response rate if you can't get the prospect to open the letter. Prospects are inundated by all types of unsolicited mailings asking them to join or buy something. When you mail a solicitation packet to prospects, you are competing with these other mailings to get the reader's attention. In order to get prospects to pay attention to your mailing you need to do something special.

Several options can be used to get prospects to open your mailings. These options include using teaser copy, using odd-shaped envelopes or special packaging, and using window envelopes.

Teaser copy is defined as some wording on the outside of the mailing envelope that is designed to draw attention to the envelope and its contents. Teaser copy usually says something like, "Important information inside!" or "Urgent message inside!" Teaser copy can be an excellent way to attract people to your piece of mail and get them to look at it instead of at all the other mail they get.

Try to be somewhat original with your teaser copy without being deceptive. When someone receives an important-looking envelope marked "Personal and Confidential" and opens the envelope to find it to be a solicitation to join an organization or subscribe to a publication, the receiver can feel somewhat offended. The contents are neither personal nor confidential. Not only are they unlikely to respond but you have also created a negative image for your organization.

The most effective teaser copy will either relate to one of the key benefits of the organization such as "Inside: Your Chance to Cut Production Costs by 25%," or will offer some type of incentive such as "Free educational opportunity inside."

Another thing to think about when using teaser copy is who is going to open the mail. In a trade association or chamber of commerce the person you are trying to reach doesn't necessarily open the mail, so putting teaser copy on the outside of the envelope is really a waste of money. Very few secretaries will see some teaser copy on the outside of an envelope and rush right in to their boss and say, "You'd better open this first."

Some organizations have tried mailing in **different colored envelopes** so their mailing will stand out in the pile of mail people get each day. In a series of mailings you might want to try at least one non-white envelope as part of your test mailings. See if it gets a higher response rate than the white envelopes do.

Odd-shaped envelopes or special packaging is a third technique which can be used to get the receiver's attention. The purpose here is to make it stand out from all of the other mail. A mailing program that worked well for one organization was sending membership materials in a small box which included a coffee mug with the organization's logo on it. The package stood out from all of the other mail and got the prospect to open it before any of the other envelopes or packages. Inside the box was a note that read "When you have your next cup of coffee, take a few minutes to read the enclosed information about us and how we can help your company. We've even provided the cup." The organization's membership staff and volunteer recruiters then made follow-up calls to the prospects to see if the cup had been received and if they could arrange to meet with the prospect to talk about joining the organization. In this case the mailing was a promotional mailing rather than a solicitation mailing because it was designed to raise the interest level of the prospect.

Window envelopes are envelopes showing the name and address of the prospect through a plastic window on the front. They are another way to get the receivers' attention since many checks and bills come in window envelopes. Another advantage of window envelopes is that they allow you to personalize the enclosed cover letter and save you the time and expense of having to address the outside of the envelope or put a separate label on the envelope because you can fold the cover letter so that the name and address fit into the window.

What to Include in the Direct Mail Package

You need to keep in mind when you are doing a direct mailing to any prospective member or group of members that in most organizations it is going to be extremely difficult to get a good response rate by just putting a brochure in an envelope and sending it. Single-piece mailings might be effective for informational mailings about educational programs. They are not effective for actually getting members to join. The key elements of any good direct mail membership solicitation package are the cover letter, the brochure, the application, a response method, and customized enclosures.

An effective **cover letter** can do several things for you. It allows you to personalize your mailing as much as possible. It lets you point out more current or specific programs or services that are going on in your organization than may be listed in your brochure. It also lets you customize your mailing toward a specific target market's needs or habits.

Since you've spent so much time and effort putting an effective **brochure** together, be sure to include it with your mailing. If you have specific brochures for specific target markets, include the appropriate ones. If you're doing repeat mailings to the same individuals or groups, you don't have to have your general information brochure in every mailing. You can coordinate your mailings so that as the cover letter varies so will the brochure you include.

You don't want to overload your package but it would certainly make sense to have a **membership application** in each package. When you have the application as a part of the brochure, it does enable you to have one less piece in the envelope. If your application is simple enough to be formatted as an attachment rather than another insert, it's worth considering this format.

If you want prospects to actually join because of what you've sent in the mail, then be prepared to make it as easy as possible for them to **respond**. If the prospect is going to be sending a check along with the application, a self-addressed, postage-paid return envelope is the easiest way to allow for that. Even if you accept credit cards for membership dues it is still a good idea to enclose the return envelope since many people don't want their credit card number showing on the outside of the application.

There are some **other enclosures** to consider. You might want to include a sample of one of your educational or informational publications to serve as an example of what the prospect will get when he or she joins. You can enclose a recent edition of your newsletter, or perhaps just a copy of an article from your newsletter that applies to something of specific interest to the individual or group of prospects to whom you're writing. One interesting technique used by a professional society was to write the message "I thought you'd be interested in this" on an article to draw extra attention to the fact that the organization had a pretty good idea of what the prospect did for a living and what information would be of interest to him or her.

Be careful about putting too much information in your mailings. If the prospect's initial reaction to the mailing is that it is an awful lot to try to read, then it's going to be difficult to get the prospect to look at everything and make a decision to join.

Quality Control Considerations

The direct mail you send to prospects is going to determine the image of your organization, so you should do everything you can within the resources of your organization to be sure you are presenting the best possible image. Some of the techniques you can use to assure the highest possible quality for your mailings are careful proofreading, evaluating and learning from mail you receive, and putting yourself on your own mailing list.

Proofreading is a skill, not just a necessary function of developing your membership materials. One of the worst "first impressions" you can make is by sending out a piece of direct mail with errors in it. Get other people to read your work before you finalize it and put it in the mail. Be sure to have someone who has never seen it before, or been involved with it in any way, evaluate each piece. Have at least two people read the material for typographical and grammatical errors.

You should also have your materials proofread by others to see if they meet the rule of common sense. Ask someone who has never seen the material before to read it and tell you if it makes any sense to them, and if the material flows easily. Try to get them to tell you if the material is clear about what you want prospects to do with the information (whether they are supposed to be more interested, as in a promotional mailing, or make the decision to join, as in a solicitation mailing).

Another quality control method to help you determine what to include in your mailings is to think about **what looks good to you**. You are a prospect for certain organizations, and thousands of products, so you know what it is that gets your attention. What other people have done successfully to get *your* interest may also work for your organization in getting prospects' attention.

Designate a file or drawer where you can keep materials you have received that had something special about them. The material got your attention, even if you didn't purchase the product or service, so it might be a technique for you to use with your prospects. Circle key points, or clip a note to the material that says "Possible for our next brochure" or "Great idea." You should also keep materials you receive that have made a negative impression on you. Put a note on these materials that says "Don't do this!"

Put yourself on **your own mailing list,** using your home address.

By the time you've had a chance to do your rough copy, sent it out to somebody to get typeset or desktop published, looked at a proof copy, sent it back for corrections, looked at it again, sent it to the printer, looked at the final draft, and sent it back to the printer, you're probably so tired of looking at it that you'll miss some of the mistakes. By putting yourself on your mailing list at your home address, you'll see your mailings with a different perspective. This might help you get a better idea of why some of the people to whom you are mailing don't respond as you thought they would. You'll also find out how fast your mailings are actually getting out from your mailing service or mailroom. This will allow you to estimate when the prospects will receive your mailing and you can start monitoring response times with some degree of realistic expectation.

A side benefit of being on your own mailing list is you'll get to see what other materials your members and prospects are receiving. Some organizations sell or rent their member lists to vendors, and you'll see what is going out to your members from these outside sources. In some larger organizations, the membership people don't really see everything that goes out to members and prospects from other departments. Being on your organization's mailing lists lets you empathize with current members and prospects, and see all of the information with which they have to deal.

Mailing your organization's membership information to prospects is one of the most basic and widely-used methods of recruiting new members. By making those mailings more effective, you raise the chances of presenting a better image to prospective members, raise the chances that they will be more receptive to a follow-up solicitation, and raise the chances that more prospects will join.

Lessons learned

- *the image of your organization is going in the mail, so spend the time and money to make that image a good one.*

- *repeat mailings are a must, so you need to budget and track those mailings.*

- *you need to do something different to get prospects to open your mailings*

- *use a cover letter and make it effective*

- *segment and target your markets to customize your mailings*

- *do some test marketing to find out what works best*

- *build quality control techniques such as proofreading into your efforts*

Chapter Ten: Telemarketing, Media, Trade Shows, and Other Recruitment Methods

What to look for in this chapter:
- *how to make the most out of using the telephone to recruit new members*
- *ways to use print and electronic media to get your message out*
- *the best way to take advantage of trade show opportunities*
- *using newer technologies in your recruitment efforts*

Recruiting new members through the mail is only one option available to your organization. There are several other recruiting methods that need to be considered. This chapter discusses some of those other recruiting options including telemarketing, print and electronic media, trade shows, and fax machines.

Telemarketing

In membership recruitment, **telemarketing** is defined as a method by which trained recruiters deliver a specific benefits message to a targeted list of qualified prospects over the telephone. It is not just a group of people sitting around a phone bank trying to contact as many people as possible in the shortest amount of time and delivering a canned sales pitch, nor is it recorded messages or untrained people calling names off of a mailing list and putting on a "hard sell" to the prospect.

Using the telephone to contact prospects has several advantages for organizations, including: the ability to make a personal contact; the opportunity to reach and to get a final decision from a large number of prospects in a short period of time; the ability to identify costs and evaluate the benefits of using this method; and the use of a technique that is less expensive than individual sales calls and provides more personal contact than direct mail. The reason telemarketing can be more effective than direct mail is that it is the first interaction with a prospect or group of prospects where the membership recruiter gets a chance to **listen** to prospects. If a telemarketer, the person making the calls, can learn to be an effective listener then he or she can be an effective telephone recruiter.

The advantage this ability to listen to prospects gives membership recruiters is that there is a tremendous opportunity to show real empathy for the prospect. In the initial phone contact, prospects typically ask several questions and sometimes mention objections to joining. If your organization relies strictly on direct mail to recruit, there is no way to answer questions or overcome objections unless you try to cover all of the possibilities in your written materials. Using the phone alleviates the need to try to anticipate and overcome every objection. If the recruiter is doing the job correctly he or she can listen to the prospect's concerns and answer in a specific, empathetic manner.

An important factor in putting together a successful telemarketing effort is selecting the right people to do the calling. Your options are the organization's staff, volunteers from among the current members, and professional telemarketing companies. There are advantages and disadvantages to all three options.

Having the **organization's staff** do the telemarketing assures familiarity with the organization, knowledge of the administrative aspects of membership, having membership materials and records easily accessible, and probably some level of experience in membership recruiting. Fulltime staff members don't have the same credibility as current members because they don't actually work in the same field or industry as the prospect. Their time constraints and possible lack of specific telemarketing experience can also be drawbacks.

If you use your **current members** to do the telemarketing you get a group of recruiters who have a lot of credibility with the prospects, can discuss specific technical or general matters related to the industry, community or field, and may possibly have personal relationships with some of the prospects. These members usually do not have telemarketing experience or training, however, and they may not be able or willing to commit much time to the telemarketing efforts.

Professional telemarketing companies offer your organization recruiters who are experienced in telephone skills and have no reluctance to try to get the prospect to join while on the phone. These people do lack the credibility of a member or staff person and don't have as much in-depth knowledge of the organization.

Regardless of which staffing option you choose you should monitor your results carefully so that you can measure the effectiveness of telemarketing versus your other recruiting methods. You should measure such things as the number of calls made per contact (to see how many calls it takes to get through to people), the average length of calls (to determine and control cost factors), and the number of prospects who joined. You should also keep track of the number of requests for more information, the average dues per new member, and the types of questions being asked by prospects. By tracking all of these areas you can better determine your return on your telemarketing dollars when compared to your other membership marketing methods. By tracking the questions being asked you can better focus your subsequent efforts.

All effective telemarketing is done using three things: a list of good, qualified prospects; an effective script or discussion guideline; and a trained sales force. Of these three things having a **good list** of qualified prospects is probably the most important. Since telemarketing is a more personal marketing approach than direct mail, it is important to take advantage of this fact by talking to people who are most likely to join. This means that your telemarketing calls should be designed to be closing calls, where your emphasis is on asking for a commitment to join. It is extremely discouraging to make dozens of calls and not get anyone to join. For the staff recruiter it's frustrating and time-consuming, for the volunteer it's demoralizing, and for the professional telemarketer it's expensive. Don't simply hand your telemarketing team a list of eligible prospects and wish them good luck. Give them a chance to be successful by providing good prospects.

Developing a good **script** or discussion guideline is important, too. The use of a script doesn't mean that the caller can't be natural and flexible in his or her responses. The main purpose of the script is to control the timing and content of the conversation so that the marketer can get to the point of asking the prospect to join without getting too far off the topic or taking too long. If you contract with a professional telemarketer to develop a script for you, be sure to put in your contract that the organization retains the rights to the script after the project is completed.

The main value that a script or outline provides is that it gives the caller help in overcoming objections. By anticipating the most frequently-heard objections to joining your organization and writing those down along with suggestions on how to overcome them, you can help the caller be more responsive without having to make something up or give a "canned" response.

Training your telemarketing team is critical to your success. For volunteers the training has to cover the four areas of organization benefits, telephone techniques, sales, and overcoming objections. The most effective way to do this is through a group training process where ideas and experiences can be shared. Role-playing and practice calls are also very helpful.

For staff members the training program might include gaining a better understanding of the prospect's work situation or specialty area. For professional telemarketers training would focus on the areas of organizational policies and benefits as well as community or profession or industry knowledge.

There is no reason why your training sessions and the actual calling of prospects can't be fun! Keep the training on a lighter level by having some competitions or giving out prizes. Of course, the best way to have fun in telemarketing is to get a lot of prospects to join!

Even though the purpose of telemarketing is primarily to gain new members there are other uses and benefits of telemarketing. They include being an effective follow-up tool to use with either a solicitation or informational mailing, being used to set up appointments with prospects during membership campaigns, being used after a personal call to reinforce what the recruiter said and add another testimonial, and allowing both the callers and the prospects to gain valuable information even if the prospect doesn't join.

Telemarketing is a viable option for most organizations as long as it is not perceived as a hard-sell technique. When used to its fullest extent and done with trained and focused personnel, telemarketing has a real place in membership recruitment.

Print and Electronic Media

Another recruitment option is placing your recruitment message in the **trade press or different publications** within your industry, profession, or community. By using the trade press you have an opportunity to reach a lot of people in a targeted way. You know you are addressing a group of qualified prospects because if they are receiving the major publications in your field, then they are already displaying interest in furthering their knowledge about their industry or profession or community. Using the trade or professional press also can give your organization additional credibility if the publication in which you put your membership message is a publication that is respected within your community, profession, or trade.

Print media membership marketing can be expensive. In order to keep the cost of print advertising down try trading space with various publications. In exchange for a one-time, one-page ad in one of your major trade publications offer the trade publication the option of putting an insert in one of your issues to your members. The trade publication gets to reach a high-profile, defined market for it's services and you get wider than normal exposure for your organization.

When running a membership ad you should be sure to include a response vehicle. This can be done by including either a detachable return postcard or using a reader response card that would be administered by the publication. As with any marketing method, tracking your effectiveness is essential.

When placing a membership ad in the trade press, you will probably have very limited space available to get your message across unless your organization can afford to buy enough space to reprint your membership brochure and application. Try to get the most important parts of your membership brochure into a format that can be used in one newspaper or magazine page. This format also lends itself well to using testimonials to get your message across quickly. If you can't reduce your application form to a size that will fit comfortably in the allotted space, you can have a place in the ad where interested prospects can check off a box and have you send them additional materials and an application at a later date.

Some larger organizations have used the electronic media of **radio and television advertising** as a means of getting their message out to prospective members. Electronic media marketing can come in the form of either the use of public service announcements (PSAs) to promote services or events that organizations sponsor or in the actual purchase of air time to place membership messages that ask people to join. PSAs are short lengths of air time that radio and television stations make available at no cost to organizations having programs or services that are for the good of the community. It is rare that a radio or television station will air an actual solicitation message for no fee. PSAs should be viewed as an opportunity to get out your promotional message rather than your solicitation message.

When placing solicitation messages with radio and television stations remember that your message has to be brief and to the point. Give the listener an address to write to for membership information or a phone number to call to join or to get additional information. A toll-free number is the best way to get prospects to respond.

Radio and television recruiting has some advantages because there is the potential to reach a lot of people with your message in a short time. The fact that your organization is soliciting members via the electronic media can be impressive to some prospects and the name recognition you gain from your messages can raise the interest of prospects even if they don't join right away. That can help set up your follow-up efforts. Keep in mind that paid recruitment messages through the electronic media can be very expensive. If you are trying to use public service announcements to raise the interest level of prospects, be aware that you don't usually get to say when the message is going to be on the air so there is a chance of missing a good portion of the particular market you're trying to reach. Unless your dues structure is very low it's hard to get people to make a quick decision to join just because of something they heard on the radio or television.

Trade Shows and Information Booths

A recruitment method that is very attractive to organizations is the use of trade show or convention booths where people can come by and actually talk to you or other representatives about joining your organization. Most industry associations, chambers of commerce or professional societies have several opportunities throughout the year to get out and meet people who are prospective members through these conventions, trade shows, or other public events. A simple, attractive booth at these shows can be a great way to meet your prospects.

Sometimes information booths aren't effective in getting people to actually join because your organization's dues are so high that it's not realistic to expect people to sign up for membership at the show site. Even in these cases, these booths can help you **qualify** your prospects and, for that reason alone, having an information booth may be worth considering as a method for marketing your organization. Qualifying your prospects means that at a trade show or convention you get the opportunity to actually talk with and listen to the prospect. You have a chance to gain additional information about her or him, and this allows you to do customized and personalized follow-up with these people after the show. Most conventions or events have some type of imprint machines or collection vehicles to gather business cards. If you are staffing one of these booths be sure to do more than just collect cards or information. Make some notes or comments on each of these contact forms and mention what the prospects said in your follow-up letter or call. This shows you were paying attention when you talked to them and suggests that this is the kind of personalized attention they'll get when they join.

There are other important points about participating in trade shows and conventions that make them important to your membership efforts. There are some events and shows that your group should attend because of the prestige of the event. If your organization is participating in the event because you expect to see prospective members, then it's pretty safe to assume that some of your current members are there, too. Invariably some of them will stop by your booth to say hello and meet the people representing their organization. Since this might be the only physical contact these current members have with your organization in the whole year, your participation in the event also becomes a retention activity.

When deciding what shows to participate in you need to look at a couple of factors. If it is a show or convention that many of your members attend then it is probably a good place for you to be since the other attendees who are not your members probably will have a lot in common with your members and qualify to join. If a show is sponsored by a major publication in your field, it is another one you should consider because the readers of that publication are probably good prospects. A final factor to consider is whether or not your members' customers, suppliers, or potential employers are at the show as attendees. If so, your organization probably needs to be there.

One place you definitely want to have a booth is at your own conventions and conferences. You'll always have some newer members attending and this is a good opportunity for them to stop by and ask questions they have about the organization. In addition, you'll almost certainly have some non-members attending and this is a chance to meet them when they are surrounded by your organization's members and materials.

In order to have a successful trade show booth, you don't have to have an expensive display of great size or one that is flashy and attracting a lot of attention. You should be sure your booth looks clean and professional, and that you have samples of just about every promotional piece your organization produces. Be sure to have plenty of applications, a lot of your basic recruitment brochures, a large supply of your magazine or newsletters, and several membership directories. There should also be a backdrop or banner of some type that indicates who you are. If you are going to spend any time talking to prospects, you should consider having some chairs or a table where you can sit and talk to the prospect as well as take notes on what information they want.

One idea to get more people to stop by your booth at your next conference or meeting is sending a notice or a flyer to non-members who are pre-registered for the meeting. Tell them if they bring the flyer to your information booth they'll get a reward, such as a free publication. It will get them into your booth and give you a chance to talk about membership.

The people staffing your booth should be a mixture of organizational staff members and current members. Current members really help establish credibility with the prospects and they can discuss specific topics of mutual interest with these prospects. Members often like working in these information booths because it exposes them to business contacts at the same time they are making membership contacts.

The costs associated with participating in these booth opportunities can vary greatly. In some local events where there is a short one-half or one day activity and most of the participants have small displays, the cost of participating can be fairly low since you don't need a large booth and one or two people can handle the assignment. There may be no need for any travel or lodging expenses. These events tend to have a low exhibitor fee.

In larger national or international events the cost can be substantial. Larger shows and conferences tend to run two to three days with as many as fifteen to twenty hours of exhibit time that needs to be covered by booth personnel. Unless the show is in your headquarters city there will be travel costs, hotel and meal costs, shipping costs, and additional materials costs to consider. On top of all this, renting space in some of the larger shows can cost several thousand dollars.

As a not-for-profit organization there are several ways to reduce the costs of participating in the larger shows. One way is get members who live in the city where the event is taking place to volunteer to work in the booth in addition to a staff coordinator. Another way to reduce costs would be to use your not-for-profit status as a negotiating tool. Many event sponsors will allow not-for-profit organizations to have booth space on a discounted or even complimentary basis as long as the materials being displayed don't compete with paying exhibitors. Consider swapping space with show sponsors. You may find that the sponsor of an event in which you want to have a booth wants an opportunity to meet your members. You can offer to exchange free space in your organization's exhibit or meeting for space in theirs.

It is sometimes difficult to know when having a booth at one of these events, especially the larger, more expensive ones, is cost-effective. It is usually not reasonable to expect a dollar-for-dollar return. It is extremely rare to sign up enough new members at an event to recoup of the costs of participating, so don't evaluate the worth of a show on the few membership applications that are likely to be received. To evaluate the effectiveness of a show or event you need to track your leads for a substantial length of time. In some cases it may be weeks, months, or even years before a person who was first introduced to your organization at a show actually joins.

Other Recruitment Options

In an age of varying communications techniques some groups have tried to be a little more interactive with their marketing efforts and have developed fax materials to communicate their recruitment message to prospective members. **Faxing** information to prospects has some appeal because people consider faxes to be more important than regular mail. This means they will probably take a little extra time reading the message because the fact that it was sent via fax shows some sense of urgency on the part of the person sending it.

If you are going to fax recruitment materials to prospects keep in mind that the quality of the materials will not be the same as if you put them in the mail. Different people and companies have different types of fax machines, and the quality of your materials is dependent upon the quality of the machines sending and receiving the faxes. Photographs and colors don't come through well on faxed messages, so just faxing a copy of your membership brochure to a prospect is not going to make that good first impression you want to make. You need to develop a recruitment piece specifically to be used with fax machines. This piece should be short, clean, easy to respond to and easy to read.

The most effective use of fax technology in membership recruitment is probably not so much as an initial solicitation piece but rather as a promotional message to raise the awareness and interest of the prospect or as a follow-up to a mailing, telephone call, personal visit, or other type of initial recruitment effort. Send a brief, eye-catching fax that tells the prospect to be looking out for an important mailing. Send this a few days before the solicitation mailing is sent. Then you can send the mailing and indicate on the outside of the envelope that this is the material the prospect was told about in the fax. You've now combined direct mail with effective teaser copy and a fax promotional message to have the prospect anticipating the solicitation.

The fax message can also be used to contact a prospect or group of prospects as a follow-up to an initial solicitation through some other format. In this case, the fax serves as reminder notice to the prospects that you want them to make a decision to join. You can also use follow-up faxes to remind prospects of any incentives that you are offering if they join right away.

Lessons learned

- *telemarketing can be an effective recruitment tool if trained recruiters are talking to qualified prospects and are listening to them*

- *print and electronic media offer opportunities to get your organization's promotional message to a lot of prospects quickly*

- *trade shows are excellent opportunities to recruit new members, qualify prospects, customize follow-up efforts and retain current members*

- *fax machines are being used more and more to get the attention of prospective members*

Chapter Eleven
Putting the "Member" Into Membership

What to look for in this chapter:
- roles that members can play in membership development
- techniques to get members involved at all levels
- identifying recruitment opportunities for members

In any trade association, professional society or chamber of commerce it is important to use all of the resources available to help the organization grow. Your organization's volunteer leadership and current members are among the most valuable of those resources.

There are a number of ways members can work with the organization's staff to create an effective membership team. One way current members can assist the organization is to go out and actually recruit new members. Even if you can't get your members to do that, you still need to work to get members to "think membership." It will help the whole organization if members and staff are dedicated to organizational growth.

In addition to recruiting others, members can help the organization's membership efforts by assisting in policy-making, gathering information, helping with retention activities, working with chapters, giving testimonials about the value of membership, and assisting in the staffing of trade show booths. This chapter focuses on how members can help in each of these areas and offers some specific suggestions on how your organization can get the most out of that help.

Probably the best way for members to have an impact on your membership efforts is to serve as **recruiters**. In a study done by the American Society of Association Executives on the recruiting techniques used in not-for-profit organizations, member-to-member recruiting was found to be the most effective way of getting people to join these organizations. While getting members to recruit others can be one of the most important parts of your membership efforts, it can also be one of the hardest parts of your efforts because of the difficulty in getting members to take on the task of membership recruitment.

It is sometimes hard to understand why people who are already members of an organization won't ask one of their peers in the community, profession, or industry to make the same commitment they've already made. When you ask members why they are reluctant to be recruiters you will likely hear them say they are too busy, or they are themselves new to the organization, or they can't think of anyone to ask. They might also say that they don't like selling, or that they don't want to pressure their friends or business associates into anything that might affect their relationship.

While all of the reasons are legitimate in the member's mind, there is probably an underlying factor in many of these reasons that is not brought out. That is that people don't want to be recruiters for your organization because they don't want to face the possibility of being rejected. It is normal for people to be reluctant to ask one of their peers to join an organization when they feel there's a good chance they'll be turned down. If you're going to utilize current members as volunteer recruiters in your membership efforts you need to train them <u>how</u> to recruit new members.

The goal in training volunteers to be more effective in membership recruitment is not necessarily to make "professional" salespeople out of them. The goal is to make them more credible as representatives of your organization, industry, profession or community by giving them confidence that they can talk to people in an educated and professional way about the reasons to join. As they develop these recruitment skills, they are also learning more about your organization and reinforcing the reasons they themselves joined.

If you are going to train your volunteer recruiters, some form of group training usually works best. When you are going to ask a group of volunteers to recruit other members during a membership campaign or on an ongoing basis, try to get this recruitment group together to talk about some of the challenges they are going to face and how they can overcome those challenges. At these training sessions you should try to get the members to do some role playing where they simulate an actual recruitment situation. By doing this you will help the members become more confident of their abilities when they have a real recruitment opportunity.

If you can't do training with groups of members at least provide volunteers with written information on how to recruit. This lets the member know that the organization cares enough about their success to give them some tools to do their job effectively.

Be sure to clarify your procedures and policies for recruiting members so that everybody involved in recruiting knows what the rules are. If this isn't done members have trouble answering questions from prospects and may give out incorrect information that is outside of organizational policy.

Try to get everybody to make a real commitment to the recruiting process by seeing three prospective members in their industry, profession or community rather than giving up after just one attempt. Prepare recruiters to overcome objections. This is the hardest challenge of recruiting and it's a challenge most volunteers are ill-equipped to face.

Giving members confidence that they actually can recruit new members can be an important first step in getting them to try to recruit for you. If you can build up that confidence then your organization has done its job in training its most effective sales force. The next step is make sure you help those volunteer recruiters identify some of the better recruitment opportunities.

The recruitment of prospects doesn't just occur during membership campaigns. Members should be encouraged to think of recruitment as an ongoing process and should be told that recruitment opportunities are always coming up. Some of these recruitment opportunities include organization-sponsored functions such as conventions, educational programs, trade shows, program meetings and social events: in the workplace where members interact with their co-workers and peers; and at gatherings of other organizations, including professional and trade groups, community groups, and other business and charitable organizations. Prospective members attend many of these functions and current members should be encouraged to talk about your organization as often as they can. Regardless of the situation, it is always good to have members who are willing and able to recruit new members.

If you can't get members to recruit at least get them to think about membership growth by **establishing policies.** Try to get your key leadership groups, such as your Membership Committee and your Board of Directors, to examine all of the policies that have an impact on membership to see if there are any adjustments that can be made to help membership growth. These policy decisions can be on topics such as whether or not your organization needs a new dues structure or dues categories, whether a dues increase is needed now or in the near future, and whether or not your organization should allow new payment options such as installment payments or payment by credit card.

Asking your members to focus on these issues can be especially helpful to your organization's efforts during difficult economic times when many businesses and professions are cutting back. There may be ways to be a little bit more creative or flexible in your structure or policies that makes it easier for those who might otherwise be reluctant to join or to maintain their membership to do so. By presenting membership issues to your leadership groups in a policy-making format you can get them involved in the membership process even though they are not actually recruiting new members.

Another way to get members involved in membership growth is by asking them to help **gather information** that can help the recruitment or retention process. Organizations are constantly concerned about knowing what their members and non-members want. If your volunteer leaders won't recruit for you then at least ask them to talk to other members. They can gather valuable information about what prospects think an organization ought to be doing for its industry, profession or community. They can also get insight from current members about how well your group is doing in meeting the needs of those who are already members.

There are several methods by which members can gather information. They can lead or participate in focus groups and gather information from current or prospective members. They can do exit interviews with members who have dropped out to find out why they are leaving and how to avoid making the same mistakes again. They can do some interviews or surveys with meeting attendees to get their reaction to specific functions. They can help put together a profile of the industry or community or profession's most important issues, so they can be addressed in membership promotional materials.

By getting members to help in this information-gathering, your organization gains the insight and data gathered and also gets more members involved in the membership process. When these members become an active part of the organization's membership team you also reassure that they are going to renew, too.

Getting members involved in **retention** is usually easier than getting them involved in selling new memberships because there is less pressure. The people they are contacting have already been "sold" on the organization so the member doesn't have to start from the beginning. It is important to remember that some of the people contacted during these retention calls will have some negative feelings about the organization so prepare your members to talk about these problems. These retention contacts can come in the form of phone calls or personal contacts or even in the form of personal notes that encourage the member to renew.

If you have a chapter structure you can get your members involved with being **chapter liaisons** on a membership level. Identify a member in each of your chapters to be the membership person in that chapter. This doesn't mean he or she necessarily has to be the person who has to recruit all of the new members in that chapter but he or she can be the person who gets information to and from the national organization and promotes membership with chapter members.

You can also get volunteers at the national or state level to go out and talk to chapters about membership. When these volunteer leaders talk to chapters on other matters such as programming or legislation, make sure they talk about membership, too. This promotion can be as simple as encouraging local chapters to participate in national membership campaigns or as forceful as actually trying to get any non-members attending the chapter meetings to join the organization.

Giving a **testimonial** for membership in an organization doesn't mean that someone has to be willing to stand up in front of a group and declare allegiance to the organization. Getting current members to endorse your group is as simple as asking permission to use their names when you are talking to prospective members, writing letters, or producing membership literature. You can also ask them to actually write a testimonial letter or you can produce one that the member can sign. Members can also provide important testimonials by calling prospects to encourage them to join, to meet with representatives of your organization, or to reinforce any points made by someone else who has already approached the prospect.

If you are using a **trade show booth** to qualify members or recruit prospects, getting your members to help staff the booth can greatly increase the chances that the show will be worthwhile. There are several reasons for having members in your booth, including the fact that they like to do it. Members also have more credibility than staff people because they can talk as a peer with the prospects. They can give an on-site testimonial about the value of membership and they will be more willing to help follow up with someone they've met.

There are any number of ways to get members involved in the membership process. Since members are among your organization's best recruiters, it just makes good sense to get them involved.

Lessons learned

- *membership recruitment and retention are most effective when current members are actively involved in the membership process*

- *members can be the best recruiters if they are trained and made aware of the many recruitment opportunities they have*

- *members can also assist membership growth by establishing membership policies, retention help, helping with chapters, prospecting, providing testimonials, and staffing trade show booths*

SAMPLE 11-A

Here is a sample of a testimonial letter sent out by a trade association. In the letter the sender uses his credibility as a dues-paying member to appeal to his peers to join.

If you own a business, to earn more you either raise prices or reduce overhead. But when you own a small business like ours, you can't afford to charge higher prices, so we're constantly looking for new ways to reduce our overhead.

When you find something really good, you just love to share the news! Well, I've found something that's too good to keep to myself - ABC.

Over the years, many organizations have tried to get us to join. They promised "savings" and "benefits". I tried a few, but I never found one that really delivered what I expected. That changed when I joined ABC, and I started to realize what I could do to help my company save money through an association.

ABC has a great, competitive insurance program, and they have a toll-free line to call with day-to-day business problems like accounting and personnel. And it's all FREE, because ABC has experts on staff to take my calls and steer me in the right direction. They also have a series of discount programs at hotels that really can save you money.

The best part of being an ABC member is their jobline. They let you know where all the work is, and that really has come in handy during these tight times. We made enough money off of our first referral to pay for three year's dues!

Since we've been getting these great benefits, and a lot more, I really thought that I had to share the good news with everyone I knew. I'd urge you to look at the ABC information that their Executive Director sent to you, and then go ahead and fill out the membership application and join. I KNOW you're going to agree that ABC membership is really worth every penny - and then some!

Sincerely,

Johnny Johnson, President
Johnson Brothers Inc.

Chapter Twelve
Membership Campaigns

What to look for in this chapter
- *the key elements of a successful membership campaign*
- *ways to organize your membership recruitment team*
- *options you can use when structuring an incentive program*

If you can get current members to actively recruit new members, then the **membership campaign** or **membership drive** can be an important recruitment option for your organization. The terms membership campaign and membership drive are used interchangeably and refer to a concentrated recruitment effort held during a specific time frame. Many organizations sponsor membership campaigns on a regular basis with the hope that they can recruit a lot of members in a very short period of time.

If your organization wants to put a successful campaign together, there are a number of key points to keep in mind. These points include getting organizational support, structuring the campaign properly, allowing adequate time to prepare, establishing clearly defined goals, deciding whether or not you will offer incentives, and having a follow-up system built into the program. Your organization should also understand all of the costs involved in the campaign and be prepared to train your recruiters. This chapter discusses all of these areas and offers specific suggestions on ways to make your membership campaigns more successful.

Before you begin a membership campaign you need to be certain that the campaign has complete **organizational support**. Make sure your volunteer leaders and all of the organization's staff know that a membership campaign is going on and are prepared to give it their full support. It's amazing how many organizations run a membership campaign in an environment where only those members and staff who are directly involved with membership feel that they have a role. Every volunteer leader needs to make some contribution to the campaign, either by being a recruiter or by paticipating in some other manner.

All of your organization's staff members should know the basic details of the campaign including the timing, who is in charge, and where to get information. The staff person charged with coordinating the campaign should prepare a brief written summary of important campaign information and distribute it to all staffers. The chief staff officer should allow time at a full staff meeting to orient the entire staff about the campaign and there should be special discussions about the campaign at volunteer leadership functions such as board of directors' meetings.

In addition to having the support of volunteer and staff leaders, you need to get the campaign **properly structured**. One person on your organization's staff needs to have overall responsibility for the campaign. This is usually the membership director if the organization has one. There should also be a volunteer leader who assumes the role of campaign chair. This could be either the volunteer membership committee chair or it could be a person assigned to chair this specific campaign. It's important to have a volunteer leader identified as head of the campaign because it gives added credibility to have someone who is a volunteer asking for that type of support from others.

If your organization has a chapter structure, it adds to the campaign's effectiveness if each chapter can identify one member who will serve as the chapter's campaign chair. This will give your organization a specific individual with whom to communicate in each chapter and adds emphasis to the campaign itself by showing that it is an important enough function to have its own specific volunteer chair.

Be certain that you are **allowing adequate time** to plan and carry out your campaign. A membership campaign put together in haste may be doomed from the outset to fail. At the very least it will not accomplish as much as it could have if the campaign were properly designed and properly promoted. When a well-publicized campaign fails, it hurts the morale of the volunteers and staff involved, it hurts the credibility of the organization, and it uses up the valuable and limited human and financial resources of the organization.

Make sure that the campaign has **clearly defined goals and objectives** that are challenging yet achievable. Many organizations sponsor a membership campaign centered on the theme "Every Member Recruit a Member." While the thought of every current member actually being able to recruit a new member is certainly a nice idea, it's not realistic. It also suggests that your organization expects to double its membership during the campaign. This really isn't an achievable goal in any membership program unless your organization is very, very small.

Membership campaign goals don't have to project huge gains in new members to be meaningful. A campaign can also be designed to increase membership in a specific geographic area, or in a specific demographic segment. Success in these campaigns might be measured by a very small number of new members, but the results might also be important to the overall objectives of your organization.

Most membership campaigns are built around some sort of **incentive program.** Incentives are special rewards given to people or companies if they join your organization during the campaign time frame. Incentives can also be given to the members who are recruiting new members, chapters or affiliates who participate in the campaign, and even staff members who participate. Incentive programs and a concentrated time frame make a membership campaign stand out from the day-to-day membership efforts of the organization.

Some of the more common incentives offered by organizations include reduced dues, prizes, gifts, free educational opportunities or publications, cash, and free trips. It is important to remember to factor the cost of these incentives into your campaign budget.

If your organization does offer an incentive to members who recruit new members during the campaign, try to structure the program so that everyone who recruits even <u>one</u> new member has a good chance of receiving something of value. If the incentive program is structured so that winning any of the awards requires recruiting more than one new member, it can appear as an overwhelming task to someone who has never recruited any new members before. A good incentive program is one that encourages new recruiters to attempt recruiting for the first time. The best way to structure an incentive program is to give recruiters a meaningful prize such as a free publication, a reduction in dues or an organizational recognition such as a lapel pin or coffee mug, for each new member recruited. In addition, that recruiter gets a chance to be entered in a drawing for a larger prize such as a free trip. For each new member recruited, the recruiter gets another chance at the larger prize. At the same time, offer a large prize for the person who recruits the most total new members during the campaign. This structure encourages members to try to recruit at least one new member to qualify for the large prize while encouraging those who are already among your active recruiters to compete for a prize for recruiting the most new members during the campaign.

When you offer incentives to prospects who *join* during membership campaigns, a word of caution is offered. Organizations frequently find that, while these incentives may be effective in getting new members to join, they can come back to haunt the organization at retention time. That's because when these same people or firms are asked to renew, the incentive is no longer part of the program.

Once a policy on incentives is established, you should try to stick to that policy. If a person must join by a certain date or recruit a new member by a certain date to qualify for an incentive or reward, your organization needs to be consistent in enforcing that deadline. If the incentives or rewards are given to those who don't meet the criteria, then the credibility of the incentive program and the organization is hurt.

During a membership campaign your organization will contact many prospective members, yet only a certain number of them will actually join. There will also be a number of prospects, who, after being approached during that campaign, are closer to joining than they were before. Your organization should have a **follow-up system** that enables someone to call on these prospects again and to try to get them to join. The follow-up contact might be made via a different format than the original contact, such as having a telephone follow-up to a campaign that was built around direct mail or personal visits. For purposes of evaluating the effectiveness of the campaign, the organization should make a record of the members that join after the follow-up contact and they should be counted as part of the successful efforts of the original campaign.

Many organizations feel a successful campaign is one that brings in a lot of members; yet, when they look back, they find out they've actually spent more money than they have gained bringing in those new members. The **cost of running a membership campaign** is more than just the promotional material developed for the campaign. Among the costs that need to be included in the campaign budget are the staff time devoted to the campaign, incentives or awards given to recruiters, incentives given to new members to join, membership literature specifically produced for the campaign, and any telemarketing or mailings.

One factor affecting the cost that is difficult to measure is the time and energy used by volunteers who were involved in the membership campaign. There is a limited amount of time members will commit to a volunteer organization and participating in a membership campaign counts against that limited time. That's why it is so important for the campaign to be organized effectively and structured so that volunteers feel they've been part of a productive effort.

By participating in a membership campaign, volunteers put themselves in a position to be rejected frequently over a concentrated period of time. If your organization is going to ask members to get involved in recruiting then you need to do everything possible to ensure the success of their efforts.

One way to do this is by **training volunteers** to recruit effectively. All campaigns should include a written guide for volunteer recruiters. This guide should explain all of the rules of the campaign and include some tips on which prospects to approach, what to say to prospects, and how to overcome objections. It should include a clear description of any incentive programs being offered during the campaign. The ideal situation is to be able to do recruiter training in person so that there can be discussions and role-playing opportunities in addition to the written materials. In larger organizations the chapters or affiliates have to do this type of training.

Another way to enhance recruiters' chances for success is to make sure they are talking to a select few of the very best prospects. Try to get volunteer recruiters to contact a limited number of well-qualified prospects during the campaign. It is recommended that newer recruiters start with no more than two or three prospects. If your organization can get your volunteers to actually recruit one of those two or three then everyone will come out ahead. The organization gets new members, the recruiter feels successful, and the new member gets the benefits of membership.

While an effective membership campaign can certainly be a big boost to your organization's recruitment program, don't count on any one membership campaign to make or break your membership efforts for the year. A membership campaign is only part of an organization's ongoing membership recruitment efforts. Even an organization with a track record of successful campaigns can't be certain that all of their future campaigns will be successful.

Lessons learned

- *well-planned and well-executed membership campaigns can add a lot of new members to an organization in a short period of time*

- *incentive programs add to the success of a campaign if they are structured to encourage members who have never recruited before to try to recruit others*

- *to assure success for your membership campaign, be sure to provide your volunteer recruiters with good recruitment materials and good prospects*

SAMPLE 12-A

This is a chart that shows the need to plan each step of a membership campaign. The dates listed reveal how important it is not to forget all of the activities necessary to carry out a successful campaign.

ACTIVITY	BY DATE
ANNOUNCE PROGRAM AND INCENTIVES	JANUARY 21
SCHEDULE 1ST COMMITTEE MEETING	FEBRUARY 1
SELECT RECRUITMENT COMMITTEE	FEBRUARY 5
HOLD 1ST COMMITTEE MEETING	FEBRUARY 12
DEVELOP CAMPAIGN LITERATURE/MAILING	MARCH 1
BEGIN P.R. CAMPAIGN	MARCH 1
SELECT SITE FOR VICTORY CELEBRATION	MARCH 1
PRINT LITERATURE	MARCH 15
HOLD SECOND COMMITTEE MEETING	MARCH 15
PROMOTE CAMPAIGN AT ANNUAL MEETING	MARCH 25
HOLD TRAINING SESSION FOR RECRUITERS	APRIL 5
SELECT PHONE-A-THON LOCATION	APRIL 7
SELECT PROSPECTS AND QUALIFY THEM	APRIL 15
HOLD PLANNING BREAKFAST	APRIL 20
DO PHONE-A-THON TRAINING	APRIL 25
MAIL PROSPECT LETTERS	MAY 5
HOLD PHONE-A-THON	MAY 20
RE-MAIL TO NECESSARY PROSPECTS	MAY 20
HOLD KICKOFF BREAKFAST MEETING	MAY 27
RECRUIT AND REPORT	JUNE 1-22
SEND THANK-YOU LETTERS	JUNE 25
SEND NEW MEMBER WELCOME LETTERS	AS RECRUITED
HOLD VICTORY CELEBRATION	JULY 8

Chapter Thirteen
Membership Retention: A Step-by-Step Approach

What to look for in this chapter:
  - *the importance of having a planned retention program*
  - *understanding the lifetime value of a member*
  - *a suggested five-step retention system*

Membership retention is the process by which organizations get their members to renew their memberships for another year. It is important for your organization to have a retention program that is planned and carried out with just as much care and energy as your recruitment program. After working so hard to recruit new members it just makes good sense to work hard to keep them.

The underlying purpose of establishing and implementing a planned retention system is to *raise the chances that the renewal invoice comes back with a renewal check!* Most organizations have several specific things they do to attain this goal, yet many don't recognize the fact that they are part of a planned retention system. To really have an impact on retention, your organization should identify the basic elements in its retention system and allocate both financial and human resources to implement those plan elements.

Having a planned system of membership retention is important to your organization for reasons beyond the obvious benefits of adding to the financial and human resources of your group. An effective membership retention program also can reduce the time spent on membership recruitment, help add to your non-dues income, and serve as a way to evaluate your current services.

In this chapter, the value of a planned retention system will be discussed in more detail and you will be introduced to a five-step retention process that you can adopt for your organization.

The importance of a planned retention system

If your organization can keep its members, it will have greater **financial resources**. Keeping members means you can *add* to your dues income as new members are recruited rather than using that income to replace members who drop out.

Having an effective retention plan also focuses on the *lifetime value* of a member. The lifetime value concept is actually very simple: your organization loses much more than a year's dues when a member drops out because, in addition to the dues that the member pays, the member also adds income to the organization through other programs and activities. To determine the member's lifetime value you need to add how much the average member would have spent on these activities to a year's dues. This is the *average gross income* your organization receives from one member in one year. This total is certainly more than one year's dues.

This is only what the member would have spent in one year; but the lifetime value concept also takes into account the length of time an average member stays in your organization. By multiplying the average annual gross income produced by one member by the number of years an average member stays in your organization you arrive at that lifetime value figure. That figure reinforces the economic impact that retention has on your organization.

A good retention program can also add to the **human resources** of your organization. Very few people join and automatically want to begin serving on committees or working in a leadership capacity. If your organization can keep members coming back, they will get involved in organizational activities and move up through the various leadership positions to become active and effective members in the organization.

Having a planned retention program can **save time** for your organization. It saves the time it would take you to replace members who have not renewed their membership with new members and it saves the time it would take you to continually try to get those members who are thinking of dropping out to renew instead.

A high retention rate allows you to **measure the effectiveness** of your current programs and services. The fact that your organization retains a high percentage of its members is a legitimate indication that you are meeting the needs of those members. On the other hand, if your organization is losing members it might be due to something other than a poor economy. It might be time to take a closer look at how well current programs are meeting members' needs.

When retention goes up, **non-dues income** frequently goes up too. When members continue to renew, it gives them an opportunity to better understand your organization's programs and services and see their value and benefit. Eventually, more and more of them will participate in these programs and this will generate additional income for your organization.

A high retention rate is actually a **good recruitment tool** because it is a great testimonial to your organization. When you are talking to prospective members about joining your organization, one of the things you can point out is the fact that a high percentage of your members come back year after year. This is a testimonial to the value of being a member of your organization and it is a great way to explain that value to prospective members.

Some organizations believe that the first step in retention is sending out renewal notices because they have to ask members to renew before they are going to come back for another year. Asking for the renewal check certainly is one of the most important steps in membership retention, but it is the **last** step, not the first one. If the first step in your organization's retention program is sending out the renewal notice, then your organization basically has a *two-step* retention program. Step one is invoicing and step two is *praying* — because all your organization is doing at this point is sending out invoices and praying that the dues will come in.

A Five-Step Program for Membership Retention

The following suggested five-step system is one that can be put in place in virtually any organization to increase the chances that members will renew year after year. These five steps call on your organization to do the following: focus on new members, establish a system of new member orientation, try to get everyone involved in some organizational activity, give some form of recognition to those who do get involved, and develop an effective renewal billing process.

Step One: Focus on Newer Members

No organization wants to give the impression of giving preferential treatment to one group of members over another. However, when you are trying to increase the overall retention rate it makes sense to do something special to retain newer members.

Studies done by various organizations, including the American Society of Association Executives and the American Chamber of Commerce Executives, indicate that first- and second-year members are the most likely to drop out of organizations, with first-year members making up the highest percentage of non-renewing members. This means many members never renew - even *one time!* Your organization needs to let new members know that they are special. Try to identify as clearly as you can why people or companies are joining. This isn't always an easy thing to do because your organization may have hundreds or even thousands of new members coming in over a very short period of time. That makes it even more important to have a system for keeping careful track of your new members and identifying why they joined.

This tracking can be done by having a space on your membership application for new members to indicate why they joined, and a place to list who sponsored them or recommended them to the organization. By going back to the referring sponsor, you can identify more specifically why the person or company joined. You can reinforce those reasons when you make your first contact with new menbers.

For these initial follow-up contacts with new members to have any real impact, they need to happen within a relatively short period of time after the member joins. Ideally this would happen within the first 30 days. In larger organizations it won't be possible to follow up individually with every new member, so you need to depend upon your chapters to do this.

Your organization should expend some additional and directed resources to keep first- and second-year members since these are the members most likely to drop out of your organization. Be sure to understand what benefits members want as they are joining and reinforce those benefits early in their first year of membership.

Step Two: Establish a New Member Orientation System

Even if your organization can identify specific reasons why people or companies are joining, you still need to follow up with your new members and let them know that, in addition to the reason they joined, there are other reasons for staying in the organization. This second step in a planned retention system is known as the **new member orientation** step. There are two ways that organizations orient new members. One way is through new member orientation meetings and the other is through the new member kits.

Holding orientation sessions for new members is a very effective way of letting new members know that they are special to your organization. You should try to bring groups of new members together to talk about themselves, about the organization and about what they expect the organization to do for them or their company.

Another important and positive aspect of holding new member orientations is the fact that new members get to see other new members. This can serve as positive reinforcement for new members because they see that they weren't the only ones who joined the organization and are reminded that they have made a good investment.

If your organization is structured so that it can hold new member orientations, make sure to use the orientation time wisely. Don't just have an orientation where one officer or staff person after another tells new members about your organization's structure and policies. This is sometimes referred to as a "talking heads" orientation. This can be a very boring experience for the attendees and really doesn't help your organization learn anything about the new members.

Spend some time talking about the individuals, their companies, and their careers. Someone should take notes as the new members talk and use the information to follow up with them on a personalized basis. You can write to them and say, "Thanks for coming to our orientation. You mentioned that you were interested in our insurance programs. Here's the information that you were looking for." It's a good way of reinforcing to a member that your organization is listening to them and is concerned about them and the company or institution they represent.

For some organizations, the opportunity to bring new members together is limited to their annual conventions or other meetings which only occur once or twice a year. If this is the case with your organization, you should still have some type of new member orientation through your local chapters or affiliates. If your organization helps chapters recruit and retain members, the chapters need to reciprocate by providing some of the personalized attention that your group cannot provide because of size.

Rather than trying to hold new member orientations as a method of welcoming new members, most organizations orient new members by sending them a **new member packet, or kit.** These new member packets are basically packages of information that are sent to new members immediately after they join the organization.

Inside these new member packets, new members will find such things as a membership plaque, a directory, a welcome letter from the president, a membership card, information about insurance programs, information about conventions and meetings, information about educational programs, three copies of the most recent newsletters, a sheet that asks the new member to sign up for a committee, and a list of who to call at the national office for more information. The fact that these new member packets are so stuffed with material is why they are sometimes known as "hernia kits." They are so heavy and full of information and materials that they give the person who delivers them a hernia!

This scenario may sound funny, but actually it's not. Organizations think that because they've put these new member packets in the mail that they have thereby oriented their new members. All they have really done is get these "hernia kits" off the shelf and into the hands of their new members. The organization is eager to meet its service goals by getting the material to the members. The new members have a different priority. They would like to to get something valuable for their dues investment. "Hernia packets" frequently meet the organization's need, but they rarely meet the new members' needs.

When people get their new member packet they look for the enclosures that will give them what they want from the organization. This means that many new members begin this mail orientation by taking two things out of the new member kit. First they take out the membership certificate or plaque and hang it up so that people will know that they've joined. The certificate gives the new member a sense of belonging and recognition and it can also be used as a marketing tool for companies. The other item that they often take out right away is the membership directory and the first thing they look for is their name. That's fine if they joined just in time to be in the directory, but most of the time people look in the directory and find they are not in it. Now your organization has a brand new member and the only things he or she has received so far are disappointment, a certificate, and maybe a hernia. Your new members have the disappointment that they are not in their association, society or chamber's membership directory right away. They have the hernia from lifting the packet that all of that new member information was in.

They take the rest of the information in the hernia kit and put it aside with the intent of reading through it when they get some extra time. In most cases, they never get that extra time. Since they really haven't been "oriented," it should be no surprise that when your organization sends the renewal notice to these members at the end of the year they don't come back. The problem is that the new member received this information in a format that wasn't conducive for them to understand exactly what it was.

If your organization uses a new member kit to orient new members, you might want to break it up and send out parts of it over the course of the year. Your organization has twelve months to get all this information into the hands of new members, so there is no need to send it all at once. Since new members are are among the most likely to drop out of the organization at renewal time, be sure to tell them from the start that they are special members. Tell them that over the next few months they will be getting a lot of information. If they have any questions, there is someplace they can call to get answers. New member packets are a necessity for many organizations but they need to be used effectively.

There is also a way to turn the new member's disappointment at being left out of the current directory into a more positive event. Instead of ignoring the fact that the new member has been left out, you can write something in the cover letter that acknowledges that you realize the new member's disappointment. The acknowledgment might say something like "As a brand new member you are not, of course, listed in the current directory. Please look closely at the attached mailing label and check to be certain that all of the information is accurate so that we can have your listing correct in *next year's* directory." Instead of being disappointed at being omitted from this year's directory, the new member is now anticipating being <u>included</u> in next year's directory. Mentally the new member is already renewing for next year!

Step Three: Try to Get Everyone Involved in An Activity

The third step in retention is one that every organization talks about but few get the opportunity to really do anything about. That step is **involvement**. When individuals or companies get involved in the activities of your organization, it is less likely that they will drop out because they view their involvement as an additional way to get a return on their dues investment. They get this return through the additional information they gather through their involvement, the business or professional contacts they make, and the additional recognition they receive.

Be careful not to equate involvement in your organization with holding a leadership position such as an officer or committee member. While these people are certainly involved in your organization's activities, it is unlikely that all of your members are involved at that level. Some of your members will never assume a leadership role but that doesn't mean they aren't involved or don't want to be involved. They just want to be involved at a level that is comfortable for them in terms of their time commitment.

As you plan and execute your retention system, think of involvement as meaning *participation in activities,* as well as leadership in the organization. The majority of your members believe that when they participate in an activity - going to a meeting, buying a publication, or accessing some on-line technical information - they are involved. Keep in mind that just because a person doesn't attend meetings or conventions doesn't mean the member doesn't feel involved.

The key to using involvement as a retention tool is to document it by developing a system that will provide you with the ability to track the activities of your members. This can be done by devising some type of code that identifies each activity or function in your organization. Whenever a member participates in any activity or function you should record that activity on your member record system or a special activity tracking system. For example, if your organization holds an educational program, some notation should made on your tracking system to identify the members who attended that program. Tracking the involvement of members allows your organization to identify who is participating and, more importantly, to pinpoint which members are not participating at all. Since members who don't participate or get involved are among those who are likely to drop out of your organization, this tracking system allows you to identify those members early in your program year. Then you can do something to get these members active *before* you have to go to the trouble of sending them a renewal notice and getting no response.

Some organizations use their member activity tracking information to identify inactive members. Then they assign somebody to follow up with each non-active member. The follow-up can be in the form of a postcard, a mailing, or a phone call from a staff member or a volunteer. This contact lets members know that the organization is aware of their activity and is concerned about whether or not they are getting a good return on their membership investment. It also shows that the organization wants to make sure that they have every opportunity to get involved. In some cases, just the fact that the organization noticed that the member wasn't participating and took the time to contact them gives the member a better feeling about the organization.

There are other benefits to tracking member activity and involvement. At the end of your program year you can assess which programs, publications, or activities have been best received by members. This information can assist your planning and budgeting efforts. In addition, you can look at the activity record of an individual member and get some idea of which programs or services that member feels are most valuable to his or her career or business. By knowing this you can target some of your marketing efforts for future programs by sending specialized promotions to those members who have a record of participating in similar programs.

Whatever system you use, be sure the information gathered through that system is used to help your organization's retention efforts. Identifying inactive members and getting them involved is an effective retention method.

Step Four: Give Some Form of Recognition to Those Who Do Get Involved

The fourth step in the retention system is remembering that every time a person or company gets involved in your organization someone needs to say, "Thank you!" to that member. Recognition for involvement is an important factor in getting people to come back year after year and be involved again. Knowing that not everybody is going to be involved at the leadership level means your organization shouldn't wait until the end of the year to give awards and thanks to those people who were involved. If your organization is tracking and pinpointing involvement, then it can recognize active members. Keep in mind that involvement and participation are the same thing to most members, so recognition for involvement also means recognition for participation.

If a member attends an educational program, your organization needs to send a follow-up letter that thanks the member for attending. When someone buys a publication, in addition to sending back the publication you should send back a brief note that thanks the member for participating in your organization. The note can also say that the material they requested is enclosed and it can remind them of upcoming programs and events such as your annual meeting or another educational program.

Each time a member gets involved, there needs to be a corresponding and appropriate thank you. Attending one meeting doesn't warrant a plaque or a gold watch, but it does warrant some sort of recognition. If your organization can get members involved in any way and remember to thank them for their participation, then you are enhancing the chances that when they receive a renewal notice it will come back accompanied by a check.

Step Five: Develop an Effective Renewal Invoicing Process

If your organization has done a good job of following the first four steps of the retention program — focusing on new members and understanding why they joined, following up with new members through a new member orientation or mailing, finding ways to get everyone involved and tracking that involvement, and recognizing member involvement at all levels — then you can mail the renewal invoice with great confidence that it will be returned with another year's dues. If you <u>haven't</u> followed the first four steps, then your renewal invoicing process merely becomes a system of bill collecting and not part of a system of membership retention.

Each organization has its own established method for sending out renewal notices and receiving the renewal dues. There are two ways to be more effective in the billing process. First, be consistent when enforcing renewal policies. Second, carefully select the enclosures you send with the renewal notice.

If your organization has **policies on renewing** you need to stick to them. The typical invoicing process starts off with your organization mailing the first renewal notice sixty to ninety days before the membership expires. Then you send a second notice thirty to sixty days later. There is often a third notice you send during the month the renewal is actually due and a first notice of overdue payment that follows shortly thereafter. There may even be a second reminder notice that indicates you are really getting serious and might have to drop the member from your organization's roster.

Think about this. Your organization has now sent five or six notices to each member asking him or her to renew. These members have been on the membership roster for several months without paying the dues. This is where the importance of having policies and sticking to them becomes clear. If your organization's policy is that at a certain point in time you must drop members from your roles, then you need to do just that.

This doesn't mean that your organization has to threaten anyone or act like an aggressive collection agency. It does mean that your renewal collection procedures should be carried out in a professional and efficient manner. If people or companies feel that they can continue to get membership benefits for several months without renewing, then there is little incentive for them to pay the dues in a timely manner. If the policies for renewing are communicated carefully to your members, then enforcement of those policies is nothing more than a good management technique.

A second thing you can do to make your renewal invoicing and collecting process more efficient is give careful consideration to what **enclosures** you send with the renewal invoice. Many organizations like to enclose a cover letter, an annual message from the president, or a list of recent organizational accomplishments because it reminds members how their money has been spent during the previous year and suggests that the organization can do this for the members again next year if they renew. Some organizations are reluctant to send this type of enclosure because they are afraid that it will distract the member from the real purpose of the mailing (which is to get the renewal statement and dues returned as quickly as possible).

Rather than sending a letter that tells what the organization has done as an enclosure with the renewal notice, you might consider sending this letter a few weeks *prior* to sending the renewal notice. Tell the members right in the letter that in a few weeks they will be getting their renewal notices and you hope they will rejoin quickly so they won't miss out on these benefits in the future. By sending this notice in advance, your organization is preparing the members for the renewal notice that is coming by getting them thinking positively about the organization. In cases in which the member is a company, sending this letter prior to the renewal invoice also creates the impression that the original renewal invoice is actually the second time the member has been asked to renew. Many companies will respond more quickly to this "second" notice than they will to the first.

Lessons learned:

- *having a planned retention system can help your organization generate more money, develop greater human resources, reduce recruitment time, add nondues income and help program evaluation*

- *the lifetime value of a member is equal to much more than one year's dues*

- *the five basic steps in effective retention plans are focusing on new members, having some type of new member orientation, trying to get everyone to participate, saying thank you to everybody who participates, and having an efficient renewal and dues collection process.*

SAMPLE 13-A
This table shows how one organization calculated the
lifetime value of a member.

Ave. dues (regular members)	$200.00
+ave. convention income/member	4.46
+ave. publication income/member	116.42
+ave. subscription income/member	73.83
+ave. professional development income/member	40.67
+ave. misc. (program services, fees, inc)	15.33
TOTAL AVERAGE ANNUAL INCOME/MEMBER	450.71
less: estimated cost to service per year	-75.00
TOTAL NET ANNUAL VALUE OF ONE MEMBER =	$375.71
X ave life of 8 years(85% annual retention rate)	X8
TOTAL NET LIFETIME VALUE OF ONE MEMBER	$3,005.68
COST OF FIRST YEAR DROP ($3,005.68-450.71)	$2,554.97
COST OF SECOND YEAR DROP	$2,104.26

SAMPLE 13-B
This is a letter sent as part of this trade association's renewal invoicing process. Note that the letter was sent prior to the invoice and mentions that the invoice will be coming shortly.

John Q. Member
112 Main Street
Beantown, MA 23456

Dear John,

As the enclosed brochure says "either you're in or you're out" That's a direct statement when it comes to your membership in the most dynamic association in the construction industry. With the end of our program year coming up in a few weeks, I wanted to write to you to let you know how much we're looking forward to having you "in" again next year.

This has been a great year for ABC. We reached our highest-ever membership, we had three of legislative issues adopted by the state legislature, and our new training program got off to a wonderful start. But what really made this a great year was the support of companies like yours.

ABC is more than dues. It's a dynamic network of contractors and professionals working together to preserve free enterprise and make this a profitable industry for everyone in it. The programs and services ABC offers are designed to meet the everyday needs of firms like yours - and mine.

Sometime next month you'll be getting your renewal notice for next year. I hope you'll get it back quickly, so ABC can continue to provide you these great money saving programs and marketing opportunities again.

I look forward to seeing your name on the list of our early renewals.

Sincerely,

Fred Frederickson,
President

Chapter Fourteen
101 Ways to Keep Your Members

What to look for in this chapter:

- *specific ways to implement the five steps of your retention program*
- *new ideas on how to be more effective in carrying out your current program*
- *how to better organize your retention program's resources*

Now for the world famous list of "101 Ways to Keep Your Members". This list of programs, activities and ideas has been compiled from suggestions made by hundreds of organizations around the world. Some of these ideas can be used by almost any organization, while others are applicable only in certain situations.

The list is organized according to the five steps in an effective retention program, and when an idea applies to more than one step you'll see a notation to that effect.

Ideas to Support the Recruitment Step:

1. **Organize your efforts into a formal retention system. (This idea also applies to all of the other steps in retention.)**
   Retention is a year-round priority and needs to be planned. Nothing is more important than viewing retention as a system or program. Any organization that is, or wants to be, successful at retention must be able to identify the specific steps it takes to increase its retention rate. In addition to having a series of activities that make up a retention program, your organization should be able to identify resources that can be allocated to help implement the program.

**2. Create a new member welcoming committee.
(This idea also applies to the orientation, involvement,
and recognition steps).**

Setting up a welcoming committee is really very simple. When
a new member joins, ask someone who is already a member to call
the new member. The member should say that they have just
learned from the organization that the person or firm has become a
new member. Then they should tell the new member what a good
investment membership has been for them and congratulate the
new member on making a great decision to join. In as little as ten
seconds the welcoming member has validated the new member's
decision to join by making that person feel more welcome in the
organization. At the same time, the member making the call now
feels more involved in the organization. The person making the call
doesn't necessarily have to be a member who is part of your
organization's leadership group. In fact, it is probably better to ask a
member who is not very active in the organization to make this
welcoming call because it gets that member involved and solidifies
their pride in their own membership.

**3. Give members a sample news release they can send to
local papers announcing that they've joined your
organization.**

In some organizations there are members who live and work in
communities where local papers are eager to get information about
the activities of businesses and professionals in their area. Your
organization can provide a news release form that new members
can fill out with the appropriate information about themselves and
the organization. Once the new member sees his or her name in the
local paper, they'll be reminded of the fine organization they've just
joined.

**4. When new members join, send directory updates on
peel-and-stick labels.**

One national organization uses this technique to send directory
updates to its members. While it is not as permanent and rewarding
for the new member as being in the printed edition of the directory,
it does point out the effort your organization is making to ensure
that the new member is getting some of the benefits of being in the

directory. In professional societies, the directory listing provides peer recognition and has networking value. In chambers and trade associations, the directory is used as a marketing tool.

5. If you are planning to introduce a new service, try to announce it just before renewal time.

Organizations with an effective planning process have the opportunity to time the introduction of new products and services to support their retention efforts. When new programs, services, or publications are being planned, you can try to time the announcement of their introduction to have the most impact on retention. Organizations should announce that the new program or service will start right after the largest number of members is due to renew. Be sure to remind members that they have to renew to take advantage of this service. Some organizations even remind members of new services right on their renewal invoice.

6. Make recruiters responsible for the first renewal, too.

Many organizations provide incentives for members to recruit other members but few offer any incentives to members who help keep members. If your organization has a sponsorship program where the recruiter is known, write to the recruiter at renewal time and let them know the new members they brought in during the past year are about to get a renewal notice. Ask that recruiter to call his or her recruits to let them know they are looking forward to having them with the organization again next year. It reminds the recruiter about his or her efforts, and helps keep those efforts from being wasted if the members they sponsored drop out a short time after joining.

7. Send a special newsletter to new members during their first year.

New members are special because they are the least likely to know everything that is going on in an organization, the least likely to be involved in a leadership position, and therefore the most likely to drop out. Several groups have developed new member newsletters that new members get throughout their first year of membership. These newsletters are basically a summary of the most important information that has been sent to them via other formats, such as newsletters or magazines, with further explanation and background. These publications usually go out three or four times during the year. New members stop receiving it as soon as they renew for the first time.

8. **Invoice your members in a way that gives them the maximum allowable tax advantage.**
   (This idea also applies to the invoicing step.)
   Having the renewal process begin prior to the end of the calendar year will allow members to have some financial flexibility. They'll appreciate your organization's understanding of their needs.

9. **Let members attend their first meeting for free.**
   (This idea also applies to the orientation, involvement, and recognition steps.)
   This might seem like a tool available only to smaller organizations or chapters that meet frequently, but it can easily be adapted to any organization. Larger organizations often replace the free meeting with a free publication or other product.

10. **Give new members a free ad or other opportunity to promote their products and services.**
    (This idea also applies to the orientation, involvement, and recognition steps.)
    Organizations that allow advertising in their publications can give new members free ad space during their first year of membership. This really shows that your organization is trying to do everything possible to promote members' businesses.

11. **Keep members' names and addresses current and accurate.**
    (This idea also applies to the involvement and recognition steps.)
    It is common courtesy and good business practice to keep your membership records as accurate as possible. This becomes even more important because members' expectations increase as they compare your organization's communications to those they receive from other sources. If virtually every organization and company that wants to sell them something can get their name correct, think of

how disappointed they'll be if your organization can't!

12. When members drop out and say they didn't get anything out of their membership, try to find out exactly what they mean.

More and more organizations are trying to identify the specific reasons why members are dropping out by surveying former members to pinpoint these reasons. When a former member says that he or she never got anything out of your organization, there is usually more to it. Your organization should prepare questions that probe beyond the surface and get to the heart of why members are leaving.

13. Be sure prospects know they can't join at the national level without joining at the local level, too.

If there is a requirement that members must join your organization at more than one level you should use this fact as a positive reason to renew. When contacting those members who are overdue on their renewal payments, be sure to highlight both the national and local benefits they are losing. A member may not be happy with local chapter service but may still renew if he or she enjoys getting the national magazine or other national services.

14. Send speakers from your national office to describe how a national membership adds value to a state or local membership.

If your organization is affiliated with a national organization try to get national level representatives to visit your affiliate from time to time. In addition to being a speaker at a local meeting, the national representative can also help retention by giving members some "inside information" about the national programs and services that they receive in addition to their local or chapter benefits. This will help create a picture of a larger benefits package.

15. Have an annual open house at your organization's offices.
(This idea also applies to the orientation and involvement steps.)

One of the most important images members get of an

organization is the image of the headquarters office. Members call or write to this office but few members get to actually see the organization's headquarters. By holding some sort of function at the main offices of your organization, you let the members see where a large amount of their money is going.

16. Send a mini-survey to members six months after they join to see how they rate your organization's service.

One educational organization called this their "six month report card." It was sent to new members halfway through their first year and asked the members to grade the organization in several service areas. Any member that rated a program below an A or B was given a phone call to get more information. Then the organization used that information to try to correct the problem. The organization was also able to spot potential dropped members by noting which new members didn't even bother to return the card. These members also got a phone call.

Ideas to Support the Orientation Step

17. Have new member orientations at a new member's place of business.

Regional and smaller organizations should take advantage of the opportunity to do more personal follow-up with new members. Your staff should visit new members at their places of business and do brief new member orientations. By doing this in the comfort of the new member's own environment, you can show the member that there is no pressure in being a member — only opportunity.

18. Have new member orientations at the organization's office.

Local chapters, chambers, and the headquarters location of organizations have an opportunity to invite new members to come to their organization's offices to receive their new member orientation. Having the orientation at the organization's headquarters limits outside distractions.

19. Have group orientations so new members see others who have made the same commitment.

Some organizations have new member orientation sessions at regularly scheduled times. One of the values of group orientations is the fact that new members are impressed by the number and stature of the other people and companies who have also just joined the organization. It reinforces to the new member that he or she made a good decision by joining.

20. Make up a form that reads, "Here's what you got for 1/365th of your dues."
(This idea also applies to the involvement step.)

This technique can be used effectively to show members that their dues investment is working for them every day. The form can be sent at anytime during the year and not just at renewal time.

21. Develop a check list to use when trying to determine why members don't renew.

Send a survey that lists the most common reasons for dropping out to those people or companies who have recently dropped their membership and ask them to check off the reasons that apply to them. Be prepared to follow-up and address each of these reasons. While a written form is not as effective as actually talking to these members, it does give the organization one more chance to reinforce the value of membership and to personalize the next contact.

22. Have a member services booth at your annual meeting or convention.
(This idea also applies to the involvement step).

It may seem to be a bit of a wasted effort to have an information booth at your own meetings, since most of the attendees already know who you are and what you do. However, this may be the only event that some of your members attend each year. It gives your less active members a chance to get updated on newer programs and services. It also allows the staff to meet face-to-face with some of the non-leaders and it gives the organization a chance to promote any new programs.

23. Create an annual slogan or theme.

It's often easier to get someone's attention if they have an image of the goals of the organization. Having an annual theme or slogan can rally the existing members around a specific program or set of objectives and create an image in the minds of those thinking about dropping. If your organization is celebrating a milestone year, that entire year can be dedicated to an anniversary theme.

24. Publish an annual report and send it to all of your members.

Publishing an annual report allows your organization to summarize all of the accomplishments from the previous year. Annual reports are part of the normal business operations of most successful companies and businesses. By issuing an annual report, your organization will show that it is being run in a business-like manner and will remind any members thinking about dropping out that they would have to give up all of the benefits listed in the report.

25. Set up a speakers bureau and arrange opportunities for speakers to talk to other organizations within your profession, community or industry. (This idea also applies to the involvement and recognition steps.)

Organizations are always trying to spread the word about their group and its activities. One of the best ways to do this is by finding speaking opportunities for your organization's leaders. Rather than handling all requests for member speakers on a case-by-case basis, you can establish a system for taking advantage of these opportunities by maintaining a speakers bureau. This is a pre-qualified group of members who are capable both in terms of knowledge and speaking ability to represent your organization internally to chapters or committees and externally to the media, potential members, and other groups. When these representatives speak, current members are instilled with a sense of pride in membership which can make a difference at renewal time.

26. At your next meeting or convention have a service fair where your committees are the exhibitors. (This idea also applies to the involvement step.)

In addition to having your regular supplier exhibitors at your next meeting or convention, have a series of exhibit booths that are staffed by volunteers and are designed to show members what each of your organization's committees or program areas is accomplishing. It's a great way for members to get a picture of the many services available.

27. Hold a new member reception at your conventions and meetings.

Whenever your organization sponsors a meeting or educational program, use that opportunity to invite new members to attend a special reception. In the case of national and state organizations with chapters, this reception provides an excellent opportunity to invite new members to meet representatives from the parent organization. These receptions are usually held prior to the start of the convention or educational program. In addition to talking about the organization and learning about the expectations of the newer members, it is also a chance to explain to the new members how to get the most out of their participation in the event.

28. Hold new member orientations at other organizational functions such as educational programs.

The idea of getting new members to attend a special new member orientation at a special time and place is wonderful, but it isn't always possible. When your organization holds a meeting or conference in a city away from your headquarters city, invite new members from that area to come to an orientation at the meeting facility just prior to the start of the function. This allows the orientation process to be brought to the members and might also encourage the new members to attend the rest of the function.

Ideas to Support the Involvement Step

29. Know the warning signs of potential dropped members and do something before you send the renewal notice.

Try to create a profile of a potential dropped member. Some of the characteristics of potential drops, such as lack of participation, late payment of dues, or no response to surveys, are easy to identify. By identifying these characteristics your organization can begin contacting the members who are likely to drop long before the renewal notice is mailed.

30. Feature a service-of-the-month in your organization's magazine or newsletter.

Each time an organization communicates with its members, there is an opportunity to remind them about the value that the organization is creating every day. In each issue of your main publication, try to highlight a specific service or program. You can feature your legislative activities in one issue and your educational programs in the next. Each service will be important for different groups of members so mentioning it reinforces the benefit for those members. At the same time you are reminding every member about that particular service.

31. Hold a retention contest.

If your members respond well to incentives and competitions consider having a retention contest among your leaders. Divide the membership roster among the organization's board or membership committee members and assign each leader to a certain number of current members. Give prizes for the leaders who renew the most members. Help them out by giving them suggestions on how they can get reluctant members to renew.

32. When important issues come up, call some of your least active members and ask them for their opinion.

It's natural for organizations to contact their leadership group when an issue of great importance arises, such as a legislative crisis, a local election, or the setting of a new standard. These issues and events are also opportunities to involve some of the organization's least active members simply by asking their opinion. When the opportunity comes up, have a list of inactive members ready to call, fax, or write and ask for their opinion on how the organization should react. The fact that the organization cared enough to contact them might make the difference at renewal time.

33. Offer plenty of member-only programs and benefits.

Your organization needs to constantly remind members of the exclusive benefits they get as regular, dues-paying members. Depending upon the legal requirements of your organization, there will be many services and programs that can be reserved for members. These programs need to be highlighted whenever possible.

34. Recognize members who reach milestone membership anniversaries.

If members stay in your organization for five, ten, twenty, or more years, they are probably not among those who are likely to drop out. When members reach one of these membership milestones, it provides two retention opportunities for your organization. First, it is another opportunity to recognize a member or group of members for their support. Doing that just solidifies their membership even more. Also, by publicly recognizing these member milestones, you inspire other members to strive to earn the same recognition by maintaining their membership, too.

35. Sponsor recognition events or social functions for the support staff of your members' businesses.

A number of groups have had success by holding functions to recognize their members' support staff. Since these support people are often the ones who control access to decision makers, it helps to have them become familiar with your organization and to think of it in a very positive way.

36. As members renew, send them a deck of cards that has the organization's logo on the back of the cards and different messages on the face of each card.

This idea was used very effectively by a chamber of commerce a few years ago. It gives you an opportunity to get 52 messages across to members. It can also be an excellent recruiting tool if nonmembers notice the unique playing cards and inquire about the organization.

37. Send an audio cassette tape along with your regular publications.

Even members who don't have time to read your regular publications will have time to listen to an audio cassette tape on their way to or from work. The National Speakers Association (headquartered in Phoenix, Arizona) sends out a cassette with each edition of their monthly newsletter. The tape is another form of continuing education and also publicizes upcoming events.

38. Create a sample *Yellow Pages* listing of your members but leave out members who haven't renewed.

Some organizations encourage members to place a group listing in the local *Yellow Pages*. Rather than just reminding late payers to renew quickly or be left out, one organization sent a draft of the organization's group ad with the late paying member's name missing. The listing had a note attached to it that indicated if the renewal was received in the next ten days their listing would be included. If not, the member was told they would be leaving the opportunity to reach nearly 150,000 potential customers to the member firms who did renew.

39. Send your annual report in the form of an audio cassette. It's easier for people to listen to the great things you've done than it is for them to read about them.

This technique worked well for a professional society in Texas. Audio cassette tapes are reasonably inexpensive. After the original recording is done, duplicates cost as little as fifty to seventy-five cents, depending upon the number of copies made. Tapes allow your organization to tell its story in an effective manner. Audio cassettes can show urgency through voice inflection, allow for verbal testimonials and they are very easy to use. Since most people will play these cassettes on the way home in their cars, they are essentially a captive audience. These cassettes also can be sent just prior to renewal time and include a description of organizational accomplishments from the previous year.

40. Be sure that the people responsible for managing the membership function are on your organization's mailing lists.

Correspondence from your organization looks quite different to the member seeing it for the first time than it does to the person who created it. By putting themselves on the organization's mailing lists, the people who are responsible for the membership operations will see things just as the member or prospect sees them. It also lets the membership people know when materials are being received as well as how they looked when received. It is important that membership staff people use their home addresses rather than the office address if they want to really see the mailings as the members do.

41. Get members involved at some level because involved members don't drop out.

Your organization needs to try to find ways to get members involved in a meaningful way without taking up too much of their time. This is especially true with newer members.

42. Have a retention committee and give it goals!

There is a need for member involvement in the recruiting process and there should also be member involvement in the retention process. Your organization should have either a separate retention committee or a retention subcommittee of your membership committee. The retention committee needs to have goals and a plan of action with very definite steps that can be taken to raise the organization's retention rate. The retention committee should be assigned to develop these steps and undertake them.

43. After you send a few written invoices begin making personal calls.
(This idea also applies to the invoicing step.)

When members fail to respond to dues notices, it isn't always because they intend to drop out for a particular reason or because they are generally disappointed with your organization. Some members just want to know if the organization cares that they are out there. A personal call to let members know they are missed can make a big difference at renewal time. Larger organizations must depend upon their chapters and affiliates to handle some of these personalized contacts.

44. If you ask a member to volunteer to do a job, make sure it's a worthwhile job!

Even the smallest volunteer jobs need to provide some sense of accomplishment for the member assigned to do them. Although there is a lot of pressure to get members involved in the organization's leadership structure, just having a title is not enough to justify the valuable time members have to give up in order to participate. Be able to pinpoint the contribution each member makes to your organization's success and be certain to mention that contribution when thanking the member.

45. Keep activity charts on members so you can identify the less active members early in the year and do something to get them involved.

Members who don't participate are the most likely to drop out, so your organization should keep track of member activity as closely as possible. By doing so it is possible to identify inactive members several months before the renewal notice is sent out. By making contacts before the invoices go out, your organization shows it is watching out for all of its members.

46. Bring your lists of least active members to leadership meetings and ask their peers to contact them. (This idea also applies to the invoicing step.)

It's an important sign to members when a volunteer leader takes the time to contact a member simply to say that the organization misses them and wants to be sure they are getting their money's worth.

47. Pay special attention to members who were the last to renew during the previous renewal period. (This idea also applies to the recognition and invoicing steps).

Keep track each year of members who pay their dues last. These are among the most likely to drop out next year. As your organization begins identifying the non-active members it needs to contact, add these late payers to the priority list.

48. Send members note pads imprinted with your organization's logo and the date of the next annual meeting or convention.

Everyone uses those self-adhering note pads to attach messages to their paperwork. This is a chance to make each time they use one of those notes a reminder of your organization's upcoming activities. Have your organization's logo and the date of your next annual meeting or convention printed on these pads and then send several to each member along with their renewal acknowledgment. They'll see that date as well as the organization's name over and over again. A side benefit is that others in their workplace will see it too. The note just might encourage a co-worker to ask about the organization.

49. Assign an officer to contact a certain number of inactive members each month.
(This idea also applies to the recruitment, involvement and recognition steps.)

To some members it seems as though the only time the organization contacts them is when it needs money, information, or support. This impression is strongest among the less active members. To alleviate some of this feeling ask board or membership committee members to make some random phone calls on a monthly basis to your inactive members. These courtesy calls will remind these members that the organization knows they're still out there and that their opinion is valued. Be sure to give members who are doing the calling something substantial to talk about, such as getting input on an upcoming legislative issue or asking the member's opinion on proposed new services.

50. Be sure nonmembers pay a substantially higher fee than members for all functions.

There are two ways to make this idea support your retention efforts. First, be sure that your organization charges more for nonmembers to participate in any of your functions or to prurchase any of your publications or materials. Second, be sure to remind your current members about this additional fee that nonmembers pay. This serves to remind members of the money they save each time they take advantage of your organization's services.

51. Get more than one person in your member firms to be active.

Just because your chamber or association's key contact leaves a company doesn't mean that the company can't be saved as a member. Your organization needs to develop a network of contacts and support within member companies that goes beyond the firm's primary representative. This can be done by adding other company personnel to your organization's newsletter or magazine mailing list, by inviting others from member firms to attend meetings or serve on committees, or by going into the company on a periodic basis to meet with management personnel to update them on your current programs.

52. Get members to attend your conventions or annual meetings.

Members who attend an organization's most important function are bound to be impressed enough to renew their membership. Even if they don't attend every year, the stature of the event and the impression they get by attending will help remind them of the benefits of membership. They will certainly have made contact with many new people at the meeting and they'll want to remain a member to assure that they will see some of these people again.

53. Hold leadership training programs to give members the tools to be successful volunteers.

It is important for members who do get involved to have a good experience during their involvement. Leadership training is becoming one of the best services that organizations can give their members. The skills developed through leadership training are transferred back to the members' workplaces. At renewal time, members and the people or companies they work for will remember where these skills were developed.

54. Hold regular town meetings where members can have an open forum to discuss anything they want with your organization's leaders.

Here's a technique that your organization can borrow from politicians. At least once a year, hold a town meeting for members to question the organization's leaders about anything and everything pertaining to the organization. Politicians have done this for years as a way to show their constituents that they actually listen to them before determining how to represent them. It's a good message to get across to your organization's members, too.

Ideas to Support the Recognition Step

55. Have the organization's staff put handwritten notes on correspondence sent near renewal time.
(This idea also applies to the invoicing step.)

People want to personalize their membership so your organization needs to help personalize it for them. Your organization's staff should make an extra effort to add a brief handwritten note to as much member correspondence as possible. Even regular form letters and cover letters that go out with publication orders can have a note at the bottom.

56. Send press releases to newspapers when groups of new members join. Include photos when possible.

In smaller communities there are opportunities to get members' names and photographs in the local papers when they join or are given some type of an award by a prestigious organization. A group photo of a number of new members receiving their membership plaques might very well be picked up by a local paper in the community where the members live or work.

57. Provide and encourage the use of logo sheets.
(This idea also applies to the recognition step.)

There are good reasons for members to want to display your organization's official logo or insignia. In trade associations and chambers of commerce, a logo can be a marketing tool for the members' businesses. In professional societies, it is a symbol that promotes peer recognition. Your organization should urge members to use the logo on their stationery and business cards, and in their advertising and promotional material.

In one organization, a former member of a trade association continued to use the organization's logo in their company's print ads. When the organization informed the former member that its policies did not allow nonmembers to use their logo for any reason, they also asked the former member if it would be less expensive to renew than to reprint all of the company's ad copy and stationery. The former member checked and indeed it was less expensive to renew than to go through that process, so the company renewed its membership. The point here was to remind the company that when you stop paying dues you stop receiving the benefits of membership.

58. Be sure to acknowledge the receipt of renewal checks just as you do new member applications.

Your organization makes a big deal when new members join by sending them welcome letters and new member kits and by putting their names in your newsletter. Yet few organizations do anything to acknowledge current members when they renew other than sending them a canceled check! Your organization should find some way to thank members each time they renew. This could be as simple as mailing a form letter or postcard. After all, these renewing members are making the same financial commitment as first-time members and they deserve some recognition.

59. Have outside speakers promote your organization.

Don't be reluctant to ask your guest speakers to promote your organization. Prepare a very short paragraph about your organization and how its activities apply to the speaker's topic. Ask the speaker to insert the paragraph into his or her presentation at the appropriate time. The fact that someone outside of your organization mentions these activities adds credibility and prestige to the organization. This is a good way to make members feel proud of their group. Hopefully, they will feel proud enough to want to keep their membership.

60. Send congratulatory notes to members when they are recognized for service to their company, community or other organization.

Your organization certainly has members who are active in other not-for-profit organizations. You also have members who perform community service. You should try to keep up with members' activities outside of your organization and, where possible, send personal notes to members who do noteworthy things in these organizations. You also can highlight their accomplishments in your newsletter. When members are recognized for these kinds of activities, it shows that the organization is interested in them as individual people or companies.

61. Have board members send dues renewal reminder notices on their personal or company stationery.

After your organization has implemented its standard renewal invoicing process and moved into more of a collection mode, try bringing in the volunteer leaders to assist with these efforts. Determine which leaders have the most influence through either personal contact or reputation with each of the late-paying members and ask that leader to send a personal note with the next invoice.

62. Reward renewal efforts as much as you do recruitment efforts.
(This idea also applies to the involvement step.)

There is nothing wrong with building in an incentive or recognition program for retention efforts. Such a program can even be integrated into your recruitment incentives by giving the member who recruits a new member some form of appropriate recognition when the new member joins, and then recognizing him or her again if the member he or she sponsored last year joins for another year.

63. List those who do renew in your publication and thank them.

"Welcome New Members" is a headline that many people see in their organization's newsletters and magazines. You need to remember that when members renew, they are making the same investment in the organization that new members are. Your organization or its local affiliates also can list the members who have renewed and say thank you to them, too.

64. Use the benefits of national affiliation as additional reasons to renew.
(This idea also applies to the involvement step.)

Organizations that are affiliated with national and international counterparts should prepare special retention information that emphasizes the benefits provided by those parent organizations. For some people, that additional scope of benefits is worth keeping.

65. If your staff visits members, ask them to visit the least active members first.
(This idea also applies to the recruitment, orientation, and involvement steps.)

Staff members in some smaller organizations get the opportunity to know all of the members and are able to make periodic visits to their members' workplaces. In larger groups or groups that are more geographically spread out, these visits can be made when the staff is traveling. In either case, the staff should use activity charts to identify the least active members. These members should be the first ones visited.

66. Offer incentives to the first members who renew.
(This idea also applies to the involvement and invoicing steps.)

Why not have a contest among your members to see who can send in their renewal dues the fastest? If competition is traditionally a part of your organization, give some type of incentive to those who renew before a certain date or are among the first to renew. This incentive could be a free publication, discounted registration fees for an event, or a reduction in dues.

67. Start a regular column in your publication to thank members for their involvement.

One organization featured a column in their monthly newsletter that was called "Tip of the Hat." This column's sole purpose was to say "thank you" to those members who had helped the organization in some way since the previous newsletter. The member's name, his or her employer or affiliation, and the specific service they had performed were all mentioned. It became the most popular feature in the newsletter because every month the members saw either their name or the name of someone they knew.

68. Recognize your members as often as possible. Be sure to thank them for their participation at each and every level.

One enterprising executive director at a professional society had a special sheet called a "thank-you-gram" made up to enable her to send notes of appreciation quickly and with some impact. Another executive had a note pad made up with a picture of a bloodhound on it along with the words, "Just trying to track you down to say thanks." It made saying thank you quick, easy, and humorous. Whether you do it formally or informally, it pays to express appreciation to members whenever possible.

69. Feature a "member of the month" in your publication. (This idea also applies to the involvement step.)

Highlighting an individual member on a regular basis is one way to assure that members who are featured will renew, as well as getting members who would like to be featured to renew. Be sure that the "members of the month" aren't all current or past organizational leaders. It's important to highlight members who do nothing more than support the organization by paying their dues on time and participating at a level that is comfortable for them.

70. When members are elected or appointed to a leadership position, send a note of congratulations to their supervisors.

In all organizations, especially in professional societies, some members have to justify the amount of time and money that is spent being a member of and participating in the organizations. Whenever possible and appropriate, your organization can send a note to the supervisors of those members who assume leadership roles in the organization. The note should recognize the member and tell the supervisor that his or her employee's involvement in your organization is accomplishing three things. It brings honor and recognition to the company or institution for which that member works, it helps the organization make a bigger contribution to the industry or profession or community, and it helps develop leadership skills in the member (who brings these enhanced skills back into the employing company or institution).

71. Get testimonials from prominent nonmembers (politicians, etc.).

Members like to hear about their organization from people outside of the organization. If the only time your organization's name is ever mentioned to a member is by the organization itself, it can cause the member to wonder about the impact and effectiveness of the organization. If you can get a prominent person from outside of the organization to mention the group and its work, it will send positive signals to members and instill a sense of pride about their membership. This can be a big plus at renewal time.

72. Give new members a special ribbon to wear. (This idea also applies to the recruitment and recognition steps.)

Identifying newer members by having them wear a special ribbon or name tag does several positive things. It lets the new member feel special and it reinforces for them the fact that joining was a good idea since there are others who have the same designation. Most importantly, it allows the organization's leaders to spot new members and try to make them feel welcome. One organization has a policy that no two officers talk to each other during a social function if there are any new members in attendance.

73. Send members a membership plaque, certificate or card each year. (This idea also applies to the involvement step.)

While most organizations send some form of membership identification to members when they first join it is just as important to send these symbols of membership to members as they renew. It is worth sending these identification pieces to members each time they renew in order to reinforce the organization's role in their businesses and careers.

74. List first-time renewals in a special section of your publication.

In addition to giving special recognition to new members, list those who are renewing for the first time in a special section of your organization's newsletter or magazine. This will remind these members that the decision they made a year ago to join the organization was a good decision. It will also remind them that the organization is glad to have them back again for a second year.

Ideas to Support the Invoicing Step

75. Call your annual fees investments rather than dues.

Referring to your organization's membership fee as an investment will create an image that your organization isn't spending the members' dues but rather is investing it in programs and services that bring value to the members.

76. When you send renewal invoices include a return envelope.

Make it as easy as possible for members to go through the renewal process. Every extra step that members must take in order to renew is one more chance for them to reconsider the membership itself. If you understand the concept of the lifetime value of a member, then the small amount of money spent to provide a return envelope is a good investment in the renewal process. Sending a postage-paid return envelope is even better.

77. Send second or third renewal notices via fax machines.

Sometimes the format of a member communication is almost as important as the message. Try sending at least one of your renewal notices via fax rather than through the mail. It shows urgency and also shows the lengths to which your organization will go to assure that the members don't lose their valuable membership benefits.

78. If your organization has a multi level dues structure, send a pre-invoice survey and bill the member based on the survey response.

Gathering information about members is as much an ongoing challenge as getting them to renew. The two efforts can be combined by sending a pre-renewal survey to members. Include the member's current listing as it appears in your records and ask them to check it for accuracy so you can be sure their renewal package is correct. The surveys that are returned will indicate the appropriate dues category for each member. Those who don't return the survey should be listed at the top of the possible drop list and get a special contact.

79. Send a letter in the form of an over-sized message pad that says "While you were out, the organization's president called about your renewal" to members who haven't renewed.

Almost every person has seen those pink "While You Were Out" notices on his or her desk. Your organization can send an oversized version with a message on it that your organization's president called and wanted to know the status of their renewal. This technique is a bit of a gimmick but it can be useful in getting the member's attention.

80. Use newer technologies to send one of your reminder notices.

As technology changes so does the way members and organizations communicate. Newer technologies often get priority attention from the members. Rather than sending another invoice through the regular mail, try putting a message on your members' electronic mail system.

81. Send members who have just dropped their membership a newsletter that only has copy on the front and back covers. Inside put a message that tells the members what they would be reading about right now if they had renewed on time.

Your organization's publications are among its most valuable membership benefits. When members drop out, they need to be reminded that they are losing these valuable benefits forever. By sending one of these publications with nothing in it except the table of contents listing all of the valuable information the former member *isn't* getting, you graphically describe the lost benefit. In corporate membership organizations, this technique can be effective because more than one person in a company is usually getting the publication. When these secondary subscribers find out they are no longer going to be getting the publications, they might contact the decision maker and ask that person to reconsider and renew the company's membership.

82. Give discounts for members who renew early.

One of the hard parts of retention is trying to figure out who among those who are late renewing is really a potential nonrenewing member and who is just putting the renewal off. One way to help resolve this problem is to give some sort of small discount for members who renew early. Your organization's financial managers need to work out the appropriate discount and accounting methods, but having the early renewal money in interest-bearing accounts may more than offset any discount given. In addition to the financial rewards for your organization, there is the main benefit of being able to identify the organization's most likely drops earlier in the renewal process.

83. Give rebate vouchers for early renewals.

Instead of giving a discount for early renewals, try giving a rebate. When you ask your members to pay the full amount at renewal time, tell them that the organization will send them a rebate voucher as a reward if they renew early. The voucher could have a monetary value or be in the form of a certificate good for a certain amount of credit when the member participates in an organizational function.

84. Accept credit cards for dues payments.

Credit card payments have become the norm for almost all purchasing transactions. If your organization does not already accept them, you should consider doing so. Credit card acceptance is especially useful to organizations during difficult economic times because it allows members to renew and still be able to make installment payments to the credit card company. Of course, the fee paid to the credit card company must be taken into consideration by the accounting people in your organization.

85. Send next year's membership renewal form already filled out and ask your members to make any necessary corrections and sign it.

In sales and marketing terminology this technique is known as an "assumed close" since it involves telling the member that your organization already knows that they are going to renew. You just want to be sure you have the correct information.

86. Send renewal notices that look like formal invitations.

When people or companies begin to take their membership for granted, there is always the chance that renewing is not high on their priority list. The invitation technique reminds the member that membership in your organization is not automatic and in fact is an honor. It is just human nature to prefer being invited to participate rather than being billed for it.

87. Have your president send a pre-invoice letter on his or her letterhead a few weeks before the invoice is mailed.

It is common for organizations to enclose a year-end report or letter from the president with their renewal notices. This is usually done to remind members of all of the value they received during the past year and to tell them what they can expect in the future. By sending the report or letter prior to the invoice you alert members that the invoice is coming and raise their anticipation level and need to respond. This usually raises the number of early renewals, giving the organization a chance to earn interest on the money that much sooner. Having the letter on the stationery of your volunteer leader adds to the credibility of the message and increases the chances it will be opened promptly.

88. Send letters that look like directory updates to people who haven't renewed. Let them know that if you get their check in two weeks this is what their listing will be.

The important part of this idea is to ensure that members realize the value of being in an organization's directory. If the directory listing is perceived as a really important benefit, your organization should take care to point out that dropping membership means losing this benefit. By sending the member's listing to him or her you can create a picture of the potential lost opportunities.

**89. Send a card with wording down one side that says, "Here's our side of the story" and list your member benefits. On the other side have an empty space and above it say "We'd like to hear yours."
(This idea also applies to the orientation step.)**

This technique is really a last resort. This should be sent just before the member has to actually be dropped from your organization's roster. Sending this type of card can be used to gather useful information about why members drop and to remind them one more time about all of your organization's programs and activities. It also presents the members with one last chance to reconsider their decision to leave.

**90. Remind members how much money they saved by participating in programs at the member rate rather than at the nonmember rate.
(This idea also applies to the involvement and recognition steps.)**

This is another example of how important it is to track the involvement of your members. One large technical society which keeps careful records on member involvement attaches a brief note to their members' renewal notices. It indicates how much money the member saved during the past year by attending meetings and purchasing materials at the member discount rate. In many cases their savings were equal to or greater than their annual dues.

91. Rather than giving members discounts or credits during the first year collect the full dues amount and hold any discounts until the first renewal.

When you offer incentives in the form of reduced dues for the first year to get members to join, this incentive can actually hurt your organization's retention rate a year later, because the incentive program doesn't apply to renewing members. Rather than giving the reduced dues incentive to members during the first year, consider giving members a discount or incentive when they renew for the first time. This way, if the member doesn't renew your organization has recouped more of its investment. More importantly, it can help retention because people and companies who are not sure about renewing may consider renewing at a discounted rate for that second year.

92. Set up your billing process so that it is most advantageous to the organization's financial management system.

Your organization's leaders need to decide what the most opportune time is to send renewal invoices. Part of good retention is setting up adequate administrative procedures to take full advantage of all programming and financial opportunities.

93. Send a mock ledger sheet listing all of the benefits you've credited to your members' accounts this year.

Encourage your members to think of their membership in terms of an investment and to think of the membership benefits as their return on that investment. Make up a statement that looks like a ledger sheet and show members all of the benefits they have been getting throughout the year. When balanced against their dues payment, the return on their investment will be substantial!

94. Bring a list of names of non-renewing members to board and membership committee leadership meetings. Create a "Ten Most Wanted" list.

Every member is equally valued, but in many instances there are specific members whose absence would hurt the organization dramatically. Some companies have a bigger impact in terms of financial support (in trade associations), in terms of prestige (with leading professionals in societies), or in terms of influence by companies with ties to local government (in chambers of commerce). Once your organization pinpoints these people or companies, you can get your leadership involved in personal contact to make sure they renew each year.

95. Write a "Last Will and Testament" that indicates the member who has yet to renew will be bequeathing the benefits of membership to his or her competitors if they don't renew.

The fact that membership in your organization can provide a competitive advantage is a fact that is often lost on members. Your organization needs to point this out to them whenever appropriate.

This technique was used by a trade association to remind those who were dropping out that their competitors, who were retaining their membership, would continue to receive these advantages.

96. If you have a policy on when you must officially terminate a membership, be sure to stick to that policy.

Organizations are always reluctant to take that final step and actually remove members who don't renew from their membership rosters. This is particularly true if they think there is even the remotest chance that the member will renew. While this is understandable it is not good management. Unless the member has been granted a special payment option by a board or other policymaking body your organization needs to adhere to whatever policy it has adopted for dropping those who have not paid their dues. Carrying non-paying members on your roster is really a disservice to those who renewed on time.

97. Send renewal notices by first class mail even if everything else goes by other mailing classes.

First class mail gets opened far more frequently than bulk mail. Regardless of how other mail is sent to members, the renewal notice should always go first class.

98. Send members a pledge card and ask them to fill it out with the name of a dropped member they'll pledge to bring back.

Send a list of people who haven't renewed to those who have renewed and ask them to contact someone they know on the list to seek their renewal. Have the member tell you who they are going to contact and get that name back to your organization's headquarters. Keep track of those who eventually renew and be sure to thank the member who contacted them.

99. Do exit interviews with dropped members. (This idea also applies to the involvement step.)

Why guess about the reasons members are leaving? Your organization should be able to review a list of dropped members and identify why they left. "Failure to pay dues" is not an adequate reason. The whole point of exit interviews is to determine *why* they didn't pay their dues!

100. Use the renewal invoice to promote other programs.

You can put the dates of your annual meeting or convention right on the renewal notice along with a thank you message to your members. This eliminates the need for a separate insert to promote the meeting and allows members to handle just one piece of paper while getting several messages.

101. Do everything you can to be one of the reasons why your members want to renew. For many members, the volunteer and staff leaders are perceived to be the association, chamber or society to which they belong. If they perceive that they have a group of dedicated, qualified staff and volunteer leaders, they'll probably be back. (This idea applies to every step in the retention process!)

Lessons learned:

- *there are numerous retention activities that can be packaged into a retention program*

- *it is important to remember that each retention idea supports one or more specific steps in the retention process*

Chapter Fifteen:
PUTTING IT ALL TOGETHER

It's amazing!

It would seem logical that if you have good instincts and some common sense you can be successful in membership work. Instinct and common sense are certainly two of the best tools you have to help you attain your goals in membership recruitment and retention, but they can't be your only tools. Putting together an effective system to attract and keep members takes a lot of work and a lot of time. It also takes a lot of skill.

Look at all of the skills you'll need to be successful in membership development. You have to attain some level of proficiency in planning, sales, customer service, marketing, delegating, listening, time management, facilitation, oral and written communications, and negotiating. In addition to these skills, it would probably help if you had some knowledge of financial management, data processing, and electronic communications, too.

If you have all of these skills membership should be easy work. If you don't have all of those skills then you need help. That help has to come in the form of a well-planned and executed membership development system.

This system has to be organized through an official membership plan and supported by a team consisting of a membership staff person or persons and an energetic and dedicated volunteer membership committee. The first step in implementing your membership system is to have a clear understanding of the real benefits of joining. You and the others involved in membership have to learn to have empathy for your members and prospective members, so that your membership recruitment and retention efforts are based on the needs of the member, not just on the needs of your organization.

Your approach to prospective members should be customized to each of your major target groups and personalized whenever possible to make the prospective members feel as though you really do understand their needs. When asking someone to join your organization you also have to determine which recruitment method or methods will work best for you. You can recruit members through the mail, by telephone, at trade shows, through direct advertising, or by getting them to participate in your organization's activities. One of the most effective ways to get new members is to get your current members to recruit them. This can be done through membership campaigns and through the ongoing work of the membership committee.

Regardless of what recruitment methods you use, be prepared for the prospective members to have a number of objections to joining. By anticipating these objections you can overcome them in a way that doesn't seem to be defensive.

Recruitment is the first step in membership growth and retention is the way to enhance that growth by keeping the members you have. After a member joins, you need to be certain that there are specific steps that are taken to keep that member. These steps include identifying why each new member joined, offering new member orientation, getting members involved, giving appropriate recognition for that involvement, and having a good system of dues invoicing and renewal processing. There are at least 101 ways to implement these retention steps.

Membership development is a timeless and universal challenge because membership is the very momentum of your organization. Everything that happens in your organization starts when a person or company joins. Everything your organization does in the future will depend upon its ability to recruit and retain members. By creating and implementing an effective membership development system, you help the organization accomplish its goals and, at the same time, you will be developing skills that can benefit you in other parts of your personal and professional life.

When you stop to think of it, being successful in membership will probably mean you will get just as much out of the membership function as you put into it.

And that really is amazing.

MEMBERSHIP DEVELOPMENT:

NOTES

NOTES

MEMBERSHIP DEVELOPMENT:

NOTES

_____

_____

_____

_____

_____

_____

_____

_____

_____

_____

_____

_____

_____

_____

_____

_____